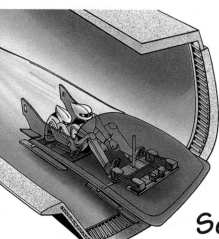

Discover HOW THINGS WORK

Contributing Writers:
Nancy Goodman
Don L. Wulffson

Elementary Education Consultant:
Anna J. Austin, Ph.D.

Technical Consultant:
Alan J. Pierce, Ed.D.

Illustrators:
Bill Whitney
Randy Hamblin

Publications International, Ltd.

Contributors:
Nancy Goodman is a freelance writer of science books and computer activities. She has worked with Chicago's Museum of Science and Industry and the Chicago Children's Museum, has developed museum exhibits, and has served as a science consultant for educational television programming.

Don L. Wulffson is the author of more than 30 books including *The Invention of Ordinary Things, Incredible True Adventures,* and *Six-Minute Mysteries.* He has authored more than three hundred stories, poems, and nonfiction pieces for children and adults.

Anna J. Austin, Ph.D., is an Associate Professor, Chairperson of the Department of Elementary Education, and Co-Chairperson of the division of Early Childhood and Elementary Education at the National-Louis University.

Alan J. Pierce, Ed.D. is an Associate Professor in the Technology Department of Elizabeth City State University and the author of the textbook *Introduction to Technology.* He writes the column "Technology Today" for the internationally distributed magazine *Tech Directions* and has served as a consultant/curriculum evaluator for the U.S. Department of Education.

Manufactured in U.S.A.

87654321

Library of Congress Catalog Card Number: 96-67889

ISBN: 0-7853-1775-9

Illustrations by: **Bill Whitney; Randy Hamblin**.

Archive Photos: 13, 74, 111, 125, 146, 157; Fotos International: 169; **Argonne National Laboratory:** 47; **Art Resource, NY:** Giraudon: 103, 183; National Portrait Gallery, Smithsonian Institution: 68; **Nicole Bengiveno/Paramount's Great America:** 59; **Bettmann Archive:** 7, 12, 14, 25, 29, 63, 71, 79, 123, 128, 129, 132, 136, 148, 150, 179, 187; **Bruce Coleman Inc.:** 97; **Photo courtesy of Contracting & Material Co.:** 36; **Culver Pictures, Inc.:** 160; **FPG International:** 48; Peter Gridley: 118; Photoworld: 16; Ron Thomas: 38; **M.L. Fuller/USGS:** 188; **Richard Hirnelsen/Medichrome:** 22; **Earl Kogler, Corporation Media/International Stock:** 131; **John F. Morgan Collection:** 60; **NASA/TSADO/Tom Stack & Associates:** 167; **Photri, Inc.:** 73, 163; **Southwestern Bell:** 117; **SuperStock:** 9, 17, 21, 87, 91, 100, 105, 115, 121, 182; Andrew Rakoczy: 84; John W. Warden: 52; **Photo courtesy of Thomson Consumer Electronics, Inc.:** 19; **Tony Stone Images:** Doris DeWitt: 172; Barbara Filet: 35; Robert Frerck: 155; Hugh Sitton: 177; **Transrapid International:** 139.

Popcorn Popper

Inside a dried popcorn kernel is starch and a little water. When the popcorn kernel is heated, the starch inside the kernel *expands*—it takes up more room. The temperature inside the *hull* (the outer covering of the kernel) gets hotter and hotter. The starch expands more and more as the temperature gets hotter until the hull breaks open. The bit of water flashes into steam. The steam creates a puff of starch and air. It's popcorn!

A hot-oil popper is one way to pop corn. Electricity flows through the *heating element*. As electricity flows, the heating element heats the pan. The pan holds oil and kernels. The pan's cover keeps the

kernels from escaping as they pop. The oil coats the popcorn and helps to heat each kernel evenly. It also keeps the popped corn from burning on the bottom of the pan.

A hot-air popper is another way to pop corn. Electricity runs a motor. The motor heats the heating element and powers a fan. Very hot air, not oil, heats the kernels evenly. The fan blows the hot air up through a screen and into the popping chamber. As the kernels pop, they become large, fluffy, and light. The hot air blows the popped corn through the chute.

popping chamber

chute

screen

heating element

fan

motor

Hot-air popper

cover

pan

heating element

Hot-oil popper

Where is most of the popcorn in the United States eaten? Ninety percent of all popcorn is eaten at home—not at the movies.

Popcorn is actually an American Indian invention. The first Europeans to try popcorn were the colonists who attended the first Thanksgiving dinner on February 22, 1630.

Food Processor

A food processor can chop, mix, blend, and slice because it uses different blades and motor speeds for each action. A motor turns the blades. The blades spin inside a covered work bowl.

A steel knife blade chops, mixes, and blends. The knife has two S-shaped blades. One blade spins near the bottom of the bowl, and the other spins half an inch higher. The bottom blade chops up the food. The top blade chops food and mixes or blends it.

Discs slice and shred. (Shredding means to cut into thin strips.) Discs are thin, flat plates. They have slots or holes with sharp edges. A disc with long slots

feed tube
work bowl
on/off switch
motor
safety switch

A few years ago, a woman filed for divorce. "The last straw was when he broke my new food processor," she told the judge. "The fool tried to mix cement in it!"

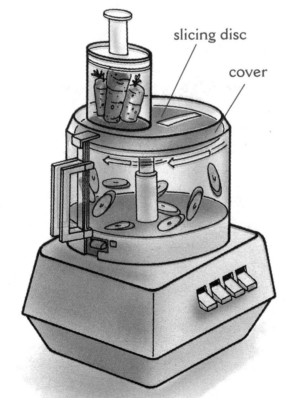

slicing disc
cover

cuts vegetables and meats into thin slices. A disc with holes shreds fruits, vegetables, cheeses, and even chocolate.

To slice a carrot, the cook places it into the *feed tube* of the processor. The cook then switches on the power. As each slot passes the feed tube, it slices off one piece of the carrot. Because the disc spins so fast, it can cut up a whole carrot in seconds.

A food processor has been built so that it is safe to use. The cover locks onto the bowl and the bowl locks onto the processor. The parts will not fly off while the processor is running. A safety switch turns off the power if the bowl or lid comes unlocked.

Toaster

Put a slice of bread into a toaster and it drops onto a *carrier*. The carrier is the rack that holds the bread in place while it toasts. A lever on the side of the toaster moves the carrier. Pushing down on the lever lowers the bread into the toaster. Pushing down on the lever also flips a switch. The switch turns on the *heating elements* inside the toaster.

The heating elements are made of wire. Electricity passes through the wire. It makes the wires so hot they glow. Toasters have one heating element for each side of the bread. These elements heat both sides of the two bread slices at once.

A *thermostat* tells when the toast is done. The thermostat is a switch that works at a certain temperature. Set the thermostat to switch off at a low temperature, and the bread will be lightly toasted. Set it to go off at a high temperature, and the bread will be darkly toasted.

When the temperature inside the toaster is high enough, it triggers the thermostat. The thermostat makes the electricity flow into a latch. The latch opens to let go of the carrier. As the carrier moves up, the heating elements turn off. The toast pops up through the slots.

Early toasters, like this one, were fancy-looking items.

In 1910, the Westinghouse Company invented an electric toaster. The first advertisements proclaimed, "Now you can have breakfast without going into the kitchen!" The idea of such a luxury caught on with the American public. Many wealthy families installed a toaster in every bedroom in the house!

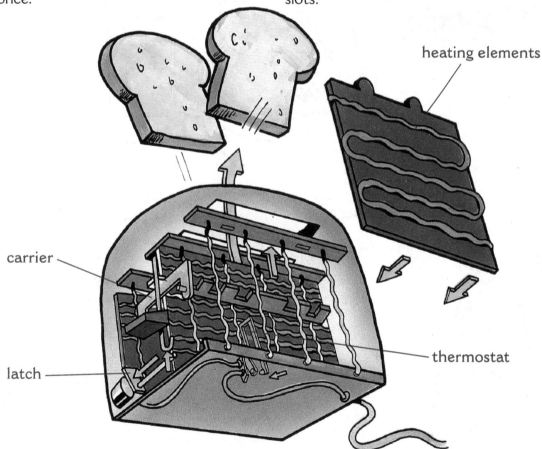

carrier

latch

heating elements

thermostat

Microwave Oven

Other forms of cooking—a flame, hot air—cook food from the outside in. A microwave oven makes the food heat itself. It cooks food from the inside out.

Microwaves pass through glass, paper, and most plastics. They bounce off metals. They are *absorbed*, or soaked up, by water and fats. Many foods are mostly made of water and fats.

Everything is made up of *molecules*. Molecules are tiny particles that are too small to see. Molecules are made up of even smaller particles called *atoms*. Different parts of atoms carry positive and negative electrical charges. One end

4. wall   3. fan   2. wave guide

1. magnetron

6. glass door

5. microwaves

of each molecule has a positive charge. The positive charges are shown here by "+" signs. The other end of each molecule has a negative charge. The negative charges are shown here by "−" signs.

The opposite ends *attract*, or pull toward each other. Positive charges pull toward negative charges. Negative charges pull toward positive charges. When microwave energy hits a molecule, the molecule tries to turn so that its charge lines up with the charge of the microwave.

Water and fats are made up of molecules.

The molecules line up their charges with the microwaves.

The movement of the molecules makes friction, and friction makes heat.

As the microwaves bounce around inside the oven, they change direction millions of times per second. This makes the food molecules turn around just as fast. The turning causes *friction*. Friction is a force created when two things rub against each other. Friction makes heat—enough heat to cook the food.

1. The microwaves are made by a *magnetron*. A magnetron is an electrical magnet.

2. The microwaves go into the oven through a *wave guide*.

3. A fan with metal blades stirs the microwaves and sends them bouncing around the oven. If the microwaves are not spread out evenly, parts of the food will be burnt and parts will be raw. Stirring the waves cooks the food evenly.

4. The walls of a microwave oven are metal. When the microwaves hit the walls, they bounce right off.

5. The microwaves that bounce onto the food are absorbed by the water and fats in the food.

6. A metal screen in the glass door protects the cook from the microwaves. Microwave ovens are built so they cannot be used with the door open.

The microwave oven did not come about as a result of someone trying to find a better, faster way to cook. During World War II, two scientists invented the magnetron, the tube that produces microwaves. Microwaves were used as part of Great Britain's radar system to spot German warplanes on their way to bomb the British Isles. Years later, it was discovered by accident that microwaves could also cook food.

Refrigerator

When you pop out of a swimming pool, you're soaking wet. Even with the sun shining on your skin, you might feel a little cool. The water on your skin is *evaporating*, or turning from liquid to gas. Evaporating takes energy, so the water on your skin pulls a little heat energy from your body. Losing heat energy means you'll feel a bit colder! A refrigerator works in the same way, by evaporating a liquid and removing heat.

Believe it or not, the ancient Greeks and Romans had a sort of refrigerator. They transported snow from mountaintops into their homes and put it into a "snow cellar." This was a hole dug in the ground, lined with logs and thick layers of straw, and packed with snow. The compressed snow turned into a solid block of ice that remained frozen for months. The ice was used to refrigerate foods.

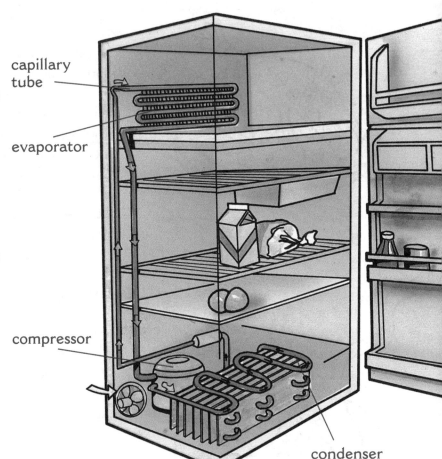

capillary tube

evaporator

compressor

condenser

Inside a refrigerator is an *evaporator*. It is made up of coils of tubing with a liquid inside. As the liquid flows through the tubing, it turns to gas and takes heat from air inside the refrigerator. That leaves the refrigerator much colder.

The gas in the tubing then runs to another part of the refrigerator, the *compressor*. There, the gas *molecules* are pressed together. Molecules are tiny particles that make up all matter.

The gas now moves through the tubes of the *condenser*. The gas molecules arrive at the condenser packed very tightly, which makes them *condense*, or change back to a liquid. When the gas

condenses, it gives off heat, which warms up the air in the kitchen.

Next, the liquid moves back up to the evaporator. To get there, it travels through the *capillary tube*, a thin tube that keeps the liquid under pressure. In the evaporator, the tubing is wider, which gives the liquid room to *expand*, or take up more space. The molecules of the liquid can spread out, changing back to gas and once again taking heat from the air in this part of the refrigerator. This liquid-gas-liquid-gas cycle repeats itself over and over, keeping the refrigerator cold.

Air Conditioner

A room air conditioner works like a refrigerator, but instead of keeping foods cold, an air conditioner can cool a whole room, or even a whole house! An air conditioner also removes *water vapor* from the air. Water vapor is tiny particles of water floating in the air. Cooler, drier air helps you feel much more comfortable on a hot day.

As in the refrigerator (see page 10), liquid in the tubes of the *evaporator* takes heat from the warm air in the room. A *blower* keeps air moving past the evaporator. The liquid pulls the heat from the air as it *evaporates,* or changes from liquid to gas. Using up the heat from the room leaves the room colder than before.

The gas is then pressed tightly together in the *compressor.* When gas is put under such pressure, it changes back to liquid. This happens in the *condenser.* Gas changing to liquid gives off heat, but this heat is blown outside so the room won't heat up again. A fan blows air over the condenser to help get rid of the heat.

When air gets colder, the amount of water vapor it can hold gets lower. The water vapor can't stay in the air, so some of it *condenses,* or changes back to a liquid. This water drips or drains off the air conditioner, leaving the air in the room cooler and drier.

In 1869, a patent was taken out on an air-conditioned rocking chair. Under the seat was a bellows. Pumping with the feet made the chair rock back and forth and sent a breath of fresh air down through a pipe above the person's head. Unfortunately for the inventor, the chair had one serious flaw: The person using it would get all hot and sweaty from pumping like crazy to cool off!

street side

fan

condenser

compressor

evaporator

blower

room side

Dishwasher

Washing the dishes is easy when you use a dishwasher. First, you load the dishes and lock the door. You turn the machine on, and a *heating element* begins to heat water. The hot water flows into the dishwasher. The soap dispenser opens to let soap mix with the water.

Next, a pump moves the hot water through pipes to the *spray arms*. The water is forced through small holes in each spray arm, so it shoots out at high pressure. This pressure makes the spray arms turn like a lawn sprinkler. It also makes the water hit the dishes in hard streams, helping to scrub the food off the dishes. The upper spray arm sprays water down, and the lower spray arm sprays it up, so the dishes are cleaned on all sides.

After the washing is done, a *valve* opens. The valve is like a door that opens to let the water out. The water is pumped out of the dishwasher.

The spray arms rinse the dishes with clear water, and the rinse water is drained out. The dishwasher may wash and rinse the dishes again. Then it is time to dry the dishes. The heating element turns on, heating the air, which makes the dishes dry faster. The hot air also kills germs on the dishes. A timer controls how long the dishwasher takes to fill, wash, rinse, and dry. When it's all over, the machine turns itself off. You open the door to find clean, dry dishes!

"If nobody else is going to invent a dishwashing machine, I'll do it myself!" proclaimed Josephine Cochrane in 1886. She was tired of her servants breaking her expensive china when they washed it. Mrs. Cochrane was soon hard at work in a woodshed next to her home. In a surprisingly short time, she had put together a dishwasher that is very similar in its design to those we use today. She patented her invention, and soon orders were pouring in from hotels and restaurants, where broken dishes were a problem. Not until the 1950s did a smaller dishwasher for the home begin to appear.

This is a 1921 version of the dishwasher.

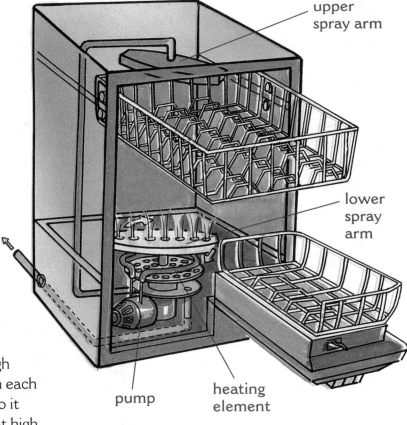

upper spray arm

lower spray arm

pump

heating element

Hair Dryer

When you dry your hair using a hair dryer, the warm air makes your hair flutter all around. Little by little, your hair becomes dry. The warm air makes the drops of water on your hair *evaporate,* or change from liquid to gas. When water evaporates, water *molecules* lift off and float into the air. Molecules are tiny particles that make up all matter.

To evaporate, water molecules need energy. The hair dryer supplies this energy in the form of heat. The warmer the air, the more quickly the water will evaporate. The stream of air also helps blow the water vapor away from your hair.

All types of hair dryers work in about the same way. Inside any hair dryer, you will find a *heating element,* a coil of wire that heats up and glows when electricity runs through it. You'll also find fan blades. A small electric motor makes the fan blades turn. The fan blades pull air into the hair dryer through the *intake vents.* Once the air is warmed up by the heating element, the fan blades blow the warm air through the *screen* at your hair. The screen keeps hair away from the heating element, so it won't get burned.

You use the switch to turn the hair dryer on and off. Some hair dryers have switches that let you run the fan blades at low or high speed or blow cool, warm, or hot air.

The first hair dryer was a vacuum cleaner! In the early 1900s, women dried their hair by connecting the hose to the back end of their vacuums. In those early models, the front end of a vacuum cleaner sucked air in and the back end blew air out. The hose could be hooked up to either end.

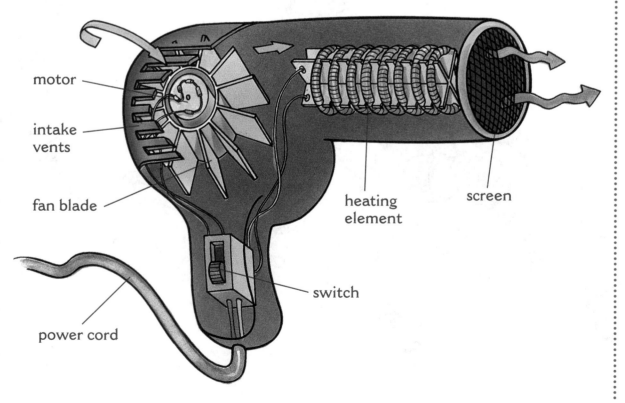

motor

intake vents

fan blade

power cord

switch

heating element

screen

Vacuum Cleaner

The first vacuum cleaner was too big and heavy to get into a house! Invented in 1901, the early vacuum cleaner was powered by gas. It weighed several hundred pounds and had to be hauled around on a horse-drawn cart. The cart was parked in front of a customer's house, and dust was sucked out of carpets and furnishings through long hoses that passed through the windows.

Vacuum cleaners come in many shapes and sizes, but they all work the same way. A motor turns a fan that pulls air into the *floor nozzle*. The air, which is filled with loose dust and dirt (and sometimes small toys!), moves through the nozzle into the hose and into the machine. The dusty air flows into the dust bag, where the dust and other particles get trapped. The air flows right through the bag because the bag has *pores,* or tiny openings. The fan keeps on pulling the air and sends it out the *exhaust,* an opening in the back of the vacuum cleaner.

The vacuum cleaner works because of *air pressure,* the force of air pressing on objects from above, below, and the sides. The fan sucks air into the machine. It creates a partial *vacuum* by reducing the amount of air under the floor nozzle. A vacuum is an area with no air in it. "Partial" means "not complete."

With less air, there is less air pressure pushing down on the dust particles. The air from the area around the partial vacuum rushes in to fill the space left by the air that was sucked into the nozzle. Dust and other objects are sucked up by the rushing air.

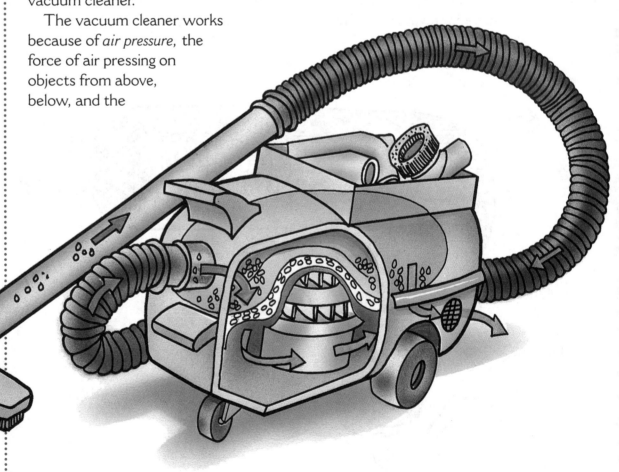

Hook-and-loop Fastener

A hook-and-loop fastener is made of two pieces of cloth tape. One piece of tape holds the hooks. The other piece holds the loops.

The hooks are really threads that are sewn into the tape. The threads are made of *nylon*. Nylon is a strong material. The nylon threads are sewn into the tape in many tiny loops. The loops are then cut open to make tiny hooks.

The second half of the fastener—the half with the loops—is made the same way. The loops are also made of nylon that has been fixed to a tape backing. Fluffy fibers, not regular loops, are sewn in. The hooks catch in these fibers.

The fastener you probably know as Velcro is a hook-and-loop fastener. In 1948, Swiss mountaineer George de Mestral was on a hike in the mountains. As often happened, he was annoyed by the thistles and cockleburs that clung to his pants and socks. While picking them off, he had an idea. He thought it might be possible to make a fastener that worked in the same way as the burs. Mestral called his invention "Locking Tape." Later, he came up with the name Velcro. "Vel," the first syllable of "velvet," was combined with "cro," the first syllable of "crochet."

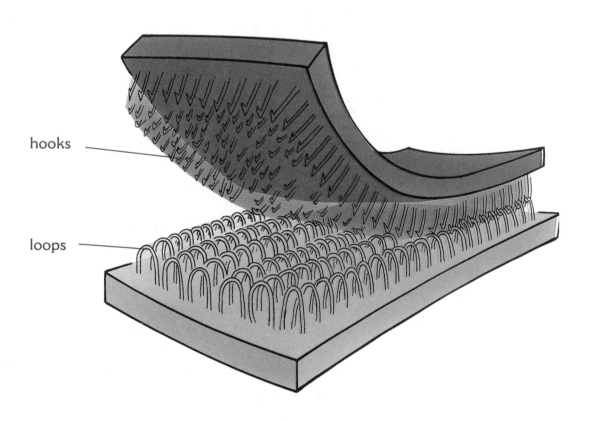

hooks

loops

Zipper

Before zippers, some garments had to fastened with many buttons.

T he teeth are the most important part of a zipper. Each tooth is a tiny bar of metal or plastic. One end of the tooth is attached to a strip of fabric. The other end of the tooth has a bump on top and a hole on the bottom. All the teeth on the strip line up. The teeth have small spaces between them.

Two strips of fabric with teeth are fastened together at the bottom so that the teeth are *staggered*. The staggered teeth make a zigzag pattern. A tooth from one strip of the zipper fits into the space between two teeth on the other strip. As the two strips come together, the bump on one tooth fits into the hole of a facing tooth. One after another, the teeth fit perfectly into the spaces.

The *slide* makes the teeth come together. The slide is Y-shaped inside. It has a *pull*. Tug up on the pull and the slide comes up. As the slide comes up, the two rows of teeth go into the top of the Y—one row on each side. The Y-shape feeds the teeth together at an angle. At the correct angle, the teeth lock

together. The teeth come out of the bottom of the slide locked together.

Tug down on the pull and the slide goes down. As the slide goes down, the row of locked teeth goes into the bottom of the Y shape. A *wedge* is in the middle of the Y. The wedge forces the teeth to unlock. The teeth come out of the top of the slide unlocked.

pull

unlocked teeth

wedge

slide

locked teeth

strip of fabric

Quartz Watch

A quartz watch uses three basic parts to keep time. The battery stores the energy. The *quartz crystal* releases the energy. The energy is released as a group of *pulses,* or beats. The *microchip* counts the pulses. The pulses must be made at an even rate—the time between beats must always be the same.

A quartz watch uses little energy. A battery may last for years. The watch never has to be wound. It keeps time as long as the battery has energy.

The quartz crystal is a part of the watch's *electrical circuit.* (A circuit is a loop.) Electricity flows in a circuit from the battery through the crystal. The flow of electricity makes the crystal *vibrate*—it moves back and forth. The crystal vibrates at a regular rate—32,768 times a second in quartz watches!

A microchip counts the back and forth movements. The microchip sends a signal to different places in different kinds of quartz watches. If the watch has a *liquid crystal display* (LCD), the signal goes to the LCD. The signal tells the LCD to add one second for every 32,768 pulses. If the watch has hands like a clock, the signal goes to a motor. The signal tells the motor to turn a set of gears every 32,768 pulses. A gear is a wheel with teeth. The gears then turn the second, minute, and hour hands.

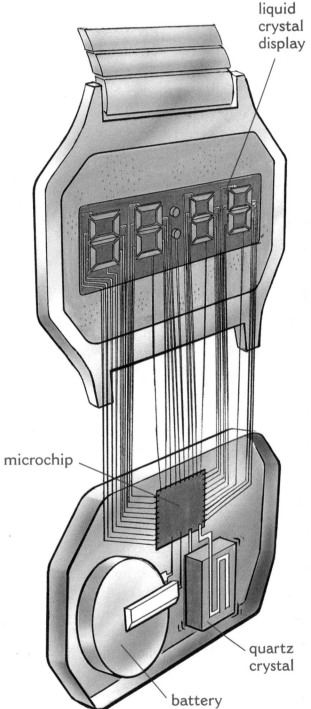

liquid crystal display

microchip

quartz crystal

battery

Wristwatches were invented in Switzerland in 1790. Originally, they were called "bracelet watches," and were only for women. The first wristwatches for men were not made until almost a hundred years later, and men who wore them were considered sissies. Not until around 1920 did wristwatches for men become accepted.

Pendulum Clock

A kind of pendulum clock you have probably seen is a grandfather clock. The pendulum clock is the grandfather of modern clocks. All clocks and watches have three basic parts. One part *stores,* or holds, energy. Another part *releases,* or gives off, the energy as a group of *pulses.* A pulse is a beat. The third part counts the pulses. For a clock or watch to keep time, the pulses must be made at an even rate.

A *pendulum* keeps the rate even in a pendulum clock. A pendulum is made up of a rod and a weight at the end of the rod. It is attached to the clock. It swings back and forth. A push starts the pendulum swinging. It takes the pendulum exactly the same time to swing back as it did to swing forth. A long pendulum takes a longer time to complete a swing; a short one takes a shorter time.

The energy to run the clock is stored by winding a gear. A gear is a wheel with pointy teeth. Winding the gear raises a heavy weight. The weight gear is connected to other gears that turn the hands of the clock.

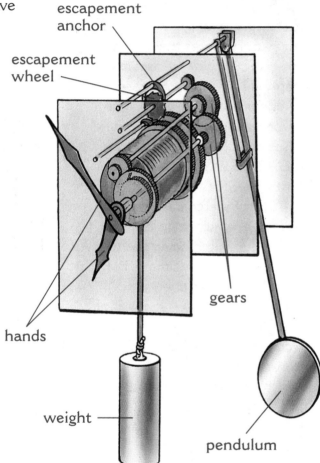

The pendulum is attached to an *escapement.* The escapement is made up of a wheel and an anchor. The *escapement wheel* has teeth on it. It is a gear. The *escapement anchor* has two ends. Each end has one point on it. The escapement controls the gear that turns the other gears.

When the pendulum swings one way, one end of the escapement anchor catches a tooth on the escapement wheel. The gears stop turning for a moment. When the pendulum swings back the other way, the anchor lets go of the tooth it was holding. It catches another tooth on the wheel with its other end. The gears turn just a little. The movement of the gears controls the movements of the clock's hands.

The weight drops a tiny bit with each swing of the pendulum. Each time the weight drops, it sends a small push through the gears and escapement. The push keeps the pendulum swinging. The clock will run until the weight has dropped as far as it can go. Winding the clock raises the weight.

A watch that runs without a battery works like a clock. A *balance wheel* acts like a pendulum. A *mainspring* acts like a weight. The mainspring stores energy when it is wound up. The balance wheel is attached to a *hairspring*. The hairspring is the watch's escapement. The escapement pulls the balance wheel back and forth, back and forth, just like the pendulum.

In 1787, a clock maker named Levi Hutchins decided that he would make a clock that "could sound an alarm." The purpose of the clock was to keep him from oversleeping, a habit that had sometimes made him late to his job. Hutchins completed his alarm clock after only a few days of thinking and tinkering. The clock was large, measuring 29 inches by 14 inches, but it worked well. Unlike many inventors, Hutchins wasn't interested in money. His only ambition was to keep himself from oversleeping. He never bothered to patent his alarm clock or build it in large numbers to make money.

Alarm clocks have come a long way since Levi Hutchins's time.

hands

hairspring

mainspring

balance wheel

escapement anchor

gears

escapement wheel

Running Shoe

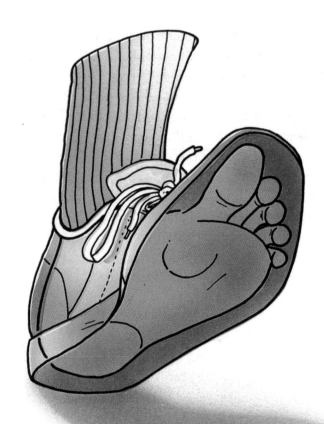

A running shoe is different from other kinds of shoes. A running shoe is designed to protect your foot during the special movements it makes when you run.

The top of the shoe that wraps around your foot is called the *upper.* It holds the shoe on your foot and keeps your foot from slipping around inside the shoe. The *midsole* is the flat inside part of the shoe that your foot rests on. It cushions your foot and helps support it as you run. The *sole* is the bottom of the shoe. The sole of a running shoe has grooves or bumps in it to keep the shoe from slipping on the ground.

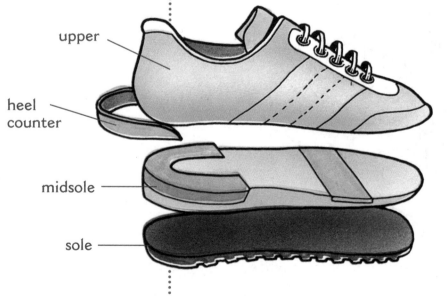

upper

heel counter

midsole

sole

A running step usually starts on the outside edge of your foot. Most runners hit the ground heel first, while a few hit the ground farther forward on the foot. Your foot strikes with a force that is about two times as much as you weigh. To protect your foot, your running shoe has padding in just the right places. This padding takes up some of the force when your foot comes down on the hard pavement. A running shoe also has a *heel counter.* This stiff plastic piece wraps around the heel and keeps it from shifting from side to side when you run.

As you continue your step, your foot rolls inward. The arch in your foot flattens out a bit. These motions probably keep your ankle, knee, and hip from having to absorb too much of the force of your step. Some people have arches that are unusually high or low.

These people often need special shoes to help the arches do their job.

In the last part of your step, your foot rolls onto the *ball,* the front part of your foot, just behind your toes. Then your foot pushes off the ground. This stage pushes the hardest on your foot—with a force about three times your weight. The shoe's padding under the ball of your foot keeps your foot from taking all this force.

In the 1960s, Phil Knight, a long-distance runner, wanted running shoes that would grip the ground better and slip less. One morning he took a waffle iron, put a piece of rubber into it, heated it, and produced a waffle-shaped pattern. Soon, Knight and a friend went into business making a new type of running shoe. The sole had waffle-shaped treads and did not slip easily. Knight called the shoes "Nike," after the Greek goddess of victory.

Now, many companies make running shoes with "waffle-type" soles.

21

Artificial Limb

Accidents or diseases can cause a person to lose a leg or an arm. When this happens, an *artificial limb* can take the place of the lost arm or leg. No artificial limb works as well as the real thing, but these devices can help people move and do many everyday tasks.

Today's artificial legs are made of special plastics and metals. They are lightweight and strong. To attach an artificial leg to the body, a person might use straps and laces. Some newer models have a *suction socket* that fits over the leg stump. It works like a suction cup to keep the leg in place.

You might not think of it when you're walking down the street, but walking is a very complicated job. For example, your knee has to bend when you step forward and then lock when you stand. Because your knee works like a hinge, an artificial knee joint has hinges to let it bend. The artificial knee joint is strong enough to hold up a person's weight, but it can move smoothly because it contains a *piston,* a sliding plug that moves up and down in a tube called a *cylinder.* The piston makes the joint move smoothly, without sudden jerks. The smooth movement of the piston helps the leg move naturally. It also keeps the knee from bending too easily so that it won't buckle when the person wants to stand still.

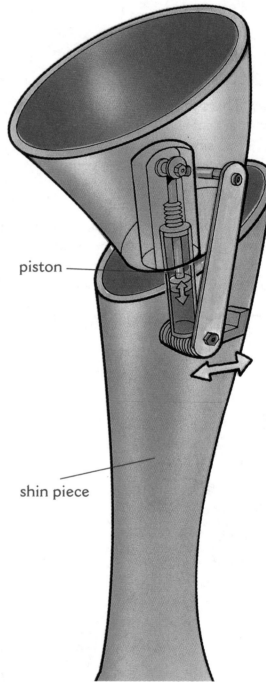

piston

shin piece

Artificial knee joint

An artificial arm can help a person pick up and lift things. The most advanced kind of artificial arm is the *myoelectric arm.* This device has *electrodes*—tiny electronic parts—that attach to a

In 1982, 17-year-old Hugh Herr suffered severe frostbite and had to have both legs amputated. But Hugh, a skilled rock climber, did not give up on himself— or his favorite sport. He built himself artificial legs just for climbing. The feet are shaped to wedge neatly into cracks and narrow ledges. With his artificial legs, Hugh still climbs some of the most difficult rock faces in the world.

Hugh Herr's artificial legs are very special. Artificial limbs also help people to perform all kinds of everyday tasks.

person's real arm or shoulder. The electrodes pick up a tiny current of electricity when the person's arm or shoulder muscle *contracts,* or squeezes together. The current turns on battery-powered motors, which turn *gears* in the wrist and fingers. Gears are wheels with teeth. These gears make the thumb and first two fingers move. The person can grip an object tightly or loosely, depending on how strongly the muscle contracts.

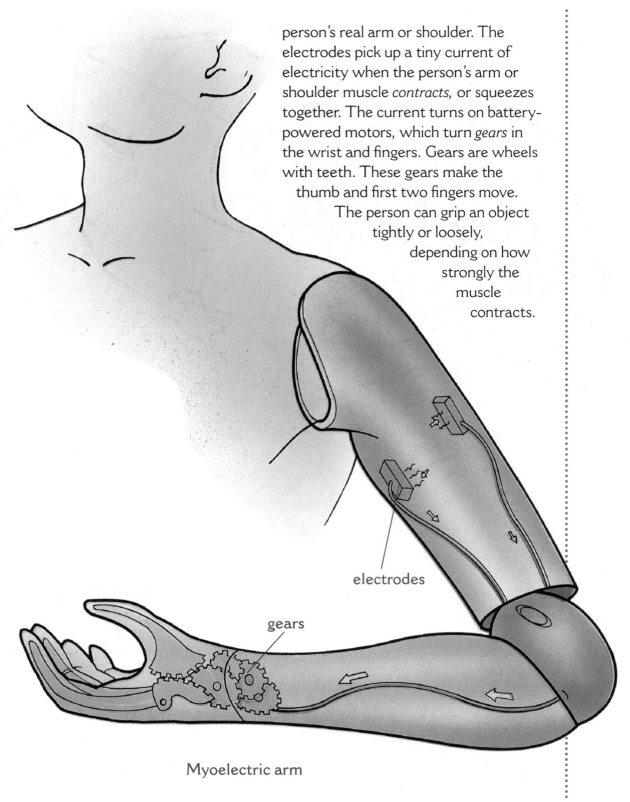

electrodes

gears

Myoelectric arm

Pencil Sharpener

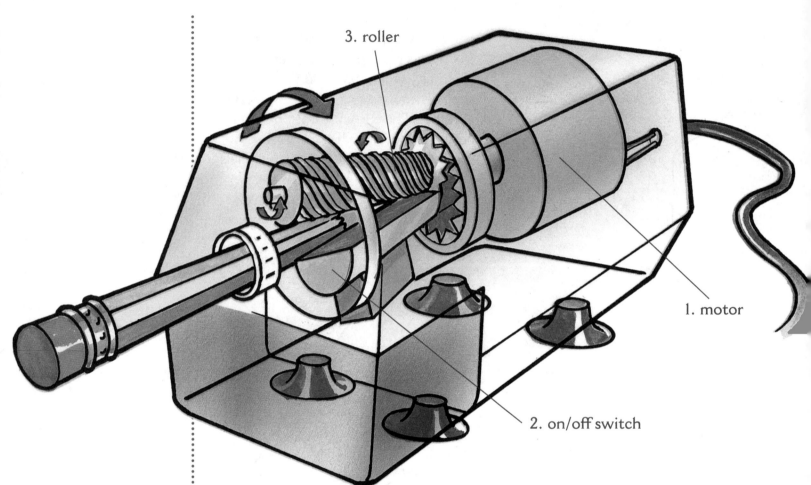

3. roller

1. motor

2. on/off switch

Electric sharpener

You've probably used several different types of pencil sharpeners. Some use electricity to work and some don't.

Electric Sharpener

1. A motor runs an electric pencil sharpener.

2. An on/off switch controls the motion of a single *roller* with spiraling, sharp edges. As the pencil is pushed into the hole, it presses the switch. The switch starts the motor, and the sharpener turns itself on.

3. The single roller shaves the pencil as it turns around in the sharpener. Pulling the pencil out stops the motor.

Crank Sharpener

1. A pencil sharpener with a *crank* uses a pair of rollers to sharpen. The rollers have raised, sharp ridges.

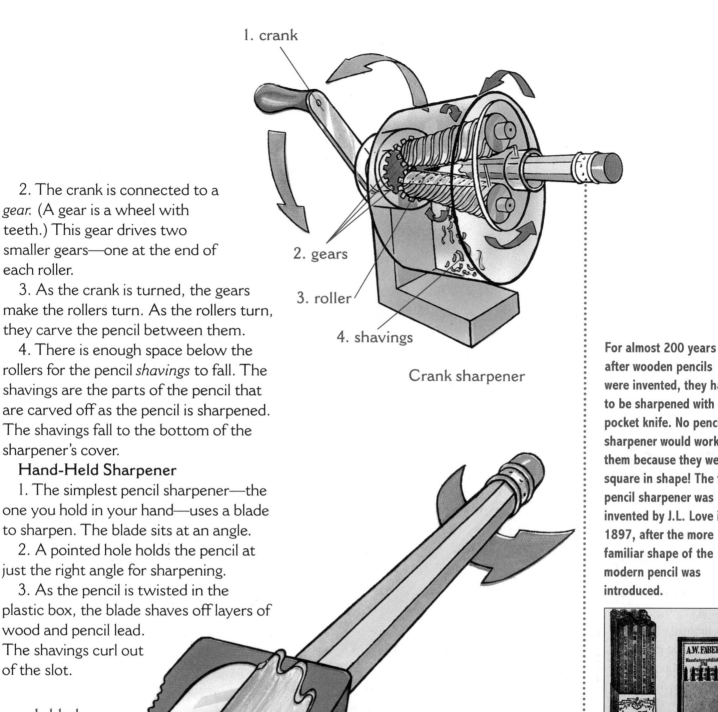

1. crank

2. gears

3. roller

4. shavings

Crank sharpener

2. The crank is connected to a *gear*. (A gear is a wheel with teeth.) This gear drives two smaller gears—one at the end of each roller.

3. As the crank is turned, the gears make the rollers turn. As the rollers turn, they carve the pencil between them.

4. There is enough space below the rollers for the pencil *shavings* to fall. The shavings are the parts of the pencil that are carved off as the pencil is sharpened. The shavings fall to the bottom of the sharpener's cover.

Hand-Held Sharpener

1. The simplest pencil sharpener—the one you hold in your hand—uses a blade to sharpen. The blade sits at an angle.

2. A pointed hole holds the pencil at just the right angle for sharpening.

3. As the pencil is twisted in the plastic box, the blade shaves off layers of wood and pencil lead. The shavings curl out of the slot.

1. blade

3. shavings

2. pointed hole

Hand-held sharpener

For almost 200 years after wooden pencils were invented, they had to be sharpened with a pocket knife. No pencil sharpener would work on them because they were square in shape! The first pencil sharpener was invented by J.L. Love in 1897, after the more familiar shape of the modern pencil was introduced.

This 1885 advertisement shows early hexagon-shaped pencils.

Lock and Key

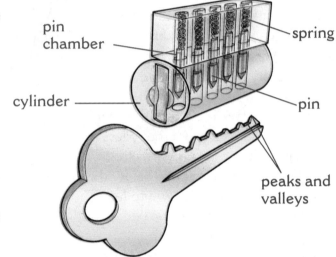

There is more than one type of lock. *Pin-tumbler* locks and *combination* locks work in different ways.

A pin-tumbler lock uses a *cylinder* and *pin chambers*. A cylinder is a tube. A row of pins connects the cylinder to the lock. The pins slide up and down. Springs push the pins down. The pins fit into holes in the side of the cylinder. When the correct key is not in the cylinder, the pins keep the cylinder from being turned. They also keep other keys from opening the lock.

Each chamber has a pin and a spring. The break between the pin and spring is different for each chamber. The breaks do not line up to make a straight line. Some breaks are high and some are low. Each key's *peaks* (the high points) and *valleys* (the low points) match the way the pins sit in the chambers. Only one key shape fits the pinning of the lock. When the right key is pushed into a lock, the peaks and valleys push each pin up just the right amount. The break in each pin lines up exactly with the top of the cylinder. The cylinder can now be turned. The lock is unlocked.

If the wrong key is pushed into the cylinder, some—but not all—of the pins may be pushed up. If even one pin is not lined up exactly with the top of the cylinder, the lock does not unlock.

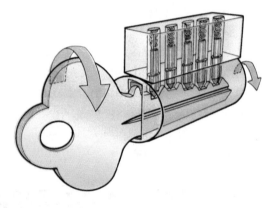

Pin-tumbler lock

A combination lock does not use a key. Three rings inside the lock turn on one *axis*. The axis is the straight line around which the rings turn. The knob and dial also turn on the axis. Each of the three rings has a notch cut into its rim that is shaped like a V or a U.

The dial has a pin on its back. As the dial is turned clockwise, the pin catches an arm on the front of the first ring. The pin makes the dial and the first ring turn

The first locks were those used by the Egyptians more than 4,000 years ago. They were made of wood, and were opened with a huge wooden key shaped like a toothbrush with a set of wooden pegs instead of bristles. The long keys were carried on the shoulder.

together. The first ring also has a pin on its back, and the second ring has an arm on its front. As the dial turns counterclockwise, the first ring turns the second ring. The same action happens between the second and third rings. After three turns of the dial, all three rings are turning at the same time. The rings are turned until each notch is lined up. When all three notches line up, the lock is unlocked.

Step 1: Each lock has its own secret number combination. If the combination is 15-25-35, turn the dial right three times and stop at the number 15. The third ring and its notch are set in the correct position.

Step 2: Next turn the dial to the left. The third ring is free of the pin from the second ring. The first and second ring turn together for two turns until the dial stops at the number 25. The notch on the second ring lines up with the notch on the third ring.

Step 3: Now turn the dial to the right, stopping at the number 35. Only the first ring moves. The notch lines up with the other two notches. The lock is open.

Combination lock

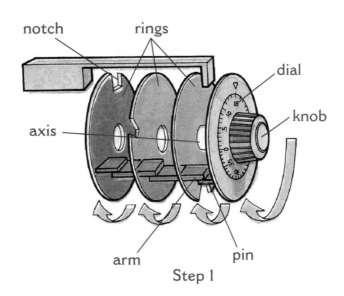

notch — rings

dial

knob

axis

arm — pin

Step 1

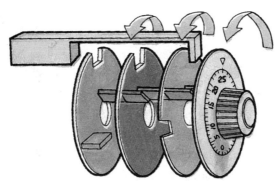

Step 2

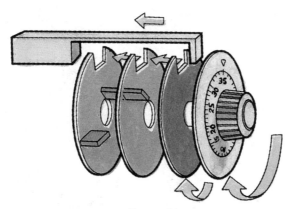

Step 3

Your school locker probably has a combination lock.

Escalator

Lift the steps out of an escalator and you'll see what looks like two huge bicycle chains and *sprockets*. A sprocket is a kind of wheel with teeth. The sprockets pull the chains. *Step axles* attach the steps of an escalator to the chains. An axle is a metal rod. Four small *rollers* on each step run in two smooth tracks. The rollers at the bottom of the step run in one metal track. The rollers at the top of the step run in another metal track. The two tracks are close to each other at the middle of the escalator's rise. They are farther apart at the top and bottom of the escalator. The difference makes the steps flatten out at the top and bottom of the rise.

A motor turns the sprocket at the top of the escalator. Because the motor can run forward or backward, the escalator runs in either direction. A belt attached to the motor turns the *drive sprocket*. The drive sprocket pulls the chain. The moving steps are all connected to the chain. As they run in a loop around the two sprockets, they carry riders up or down.

The "up" escalator steps slip from under the *combplate*. Each step then begins to rise. The two rollers on the front of each step ride the track on the outside. The two rollers on the back of each step ride the track on the inside. Because the inside track is below the outside track, the steps flatten out at the top of the escalator. The steps slip under the combplate at the top of the escalator and then loop back down.

step axles

rollers

combplate

rollers

sprocket

chain

drive sprocket

upside-down step

outside track

inside track

Invented by Jesse Reno and patented in 1892, the first escalator was simply a moving wooden stairway. Because people were afraid of escalators, an attendant was positioned at the top, ready to give smelling salts to ladies and gentlemen overcome by the experience.

To ride the earliest escalators, like this one in Paris, France, you had to pay a fee.

Elevator

Pulleys make an elevator go up and down. A pulley is a wheel with a groove. A cable—a thick rope made of wire—fits in the groove and runs around the wheel. Pulleys help raise and lower heavy objects. Pulling down on one end of the cable, for example, raises an object on the other end of the cable.

One pulley and cable could not lift an elevator. An elevator has to have many pulleys and cables. The pulleys are connected to a powerful electric motor. The elevator *cab*—the part you ride in—hangs from steel cables. Each cable runs around its own pulley.

At the other end of the cables is a *counterweight*. The counterweight is a heavy object that weighs almost as much as the elevator. The counterweight helps raise and lower the elevator. The motor has to carry only the difference between the weight of the elevator and the weight of the counterweight.

Pressing a floor button starts the motor. The motor starts turning the pulleys. The turning pulleys pull on the cables. The cables raise or lower the elevator. The elevator stops at the floor you picked.

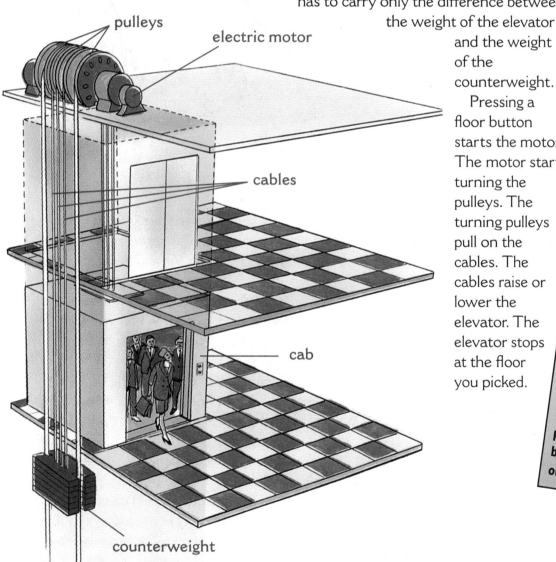

pulleys

electric motor

cables

cab

counterweight

In the Coliseum in ancient Rome, there were elevators to take the gladiators up to the arena from the basement. Basically, they were simple lifting platforms raised by pulleys. These primitive elevators were powered by humans or animals.

UP

Automatic Door

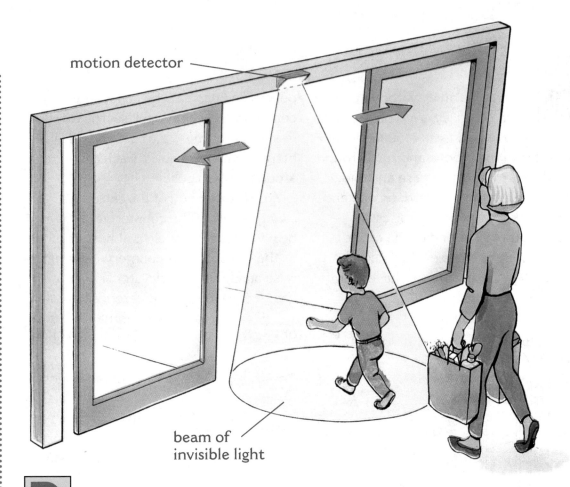

motion detector

beam of
invisible light

Albert Einstein came up with the idea for the electronic eye in 1921. Later, other scientists used his research to help them with their inventions. Today, some electronic eyes can "see" such fast-moving objects as a bullet in flight.

Doors that open *automatically,* or on their own, are a useful invention. They make it easier to leave a store with your arms full.

Some automatic doors use a *motion detector* to sense that you are getting near the door. The detector picks up nearby movement. It is placed over the door. It sends out a beam of invisible light that shines on the floor. When you step into the beam of light, the beam bounces off you, back to the motion detector. The detector then sends a signal that opens the door. When there is no movement, the doors stay closed.

Other automatic doors "see" you with many electronic eyes. One part of each

eye sends out a beam of light. The light shines across the doorway. The other part of each eye is a *light detector* that can sense the beam of light. As long as the light detector sees the beam, the door stays closed. When you step into the beam, you stop the light from reaching the light detector. The blocked light is a signal to open the door.

Some automatic doors do not use electronic eyes. Elevator doors open with the push of a button. The rubber mat in front of some supermarket doors is like a giant push button.

All these doors open electrically. Electricity powers the motors that open and close the doors. A timer holds the door open for a few seconds so you can pass through.

Automatic doors open in different ways. They can swing open. Most doors in a house swing open. Automatic doors also can slide into the wall. Elevator doors slide into the wall.

The swinging door has a motor with an "arm" attached to the top of the door. As the motor turns, it moves the arm. As the arm moves, it opens the door.

On sliding doors, a motor turns a *drive sprocket*. A sprocket is a wheel with pointy teeth. *Brackets* connect a chain to each door. The sprocket's teeth fit into a chain the same way the gear teeth of a bicycle sprocket fit into a bike chain. The chain is a loop. It moves around the drive sprocket and another sprocket at the opposite end of the loop. As the motor turns, the chain pulls the doors open. The drive sprocket reverses directions to close the doors.

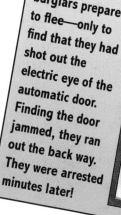

In 1983 in Berlin, Germany, a man and a woman entered a jewelry store. They both took out pistols. The man shot out what he believed to be the security camera. After filling their sacks with goodies, the burglars prepared to flee—only to find that they had shot out the electric eye of the automatic door. Finding the door jammed, they ran out the back way. They were arrested minutes later!

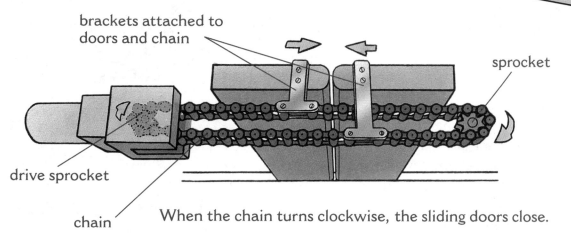

brackets attached to doors and chain

sprocket

drive sprocket

chain

When the chain turns clockwise, the sliding doors close.

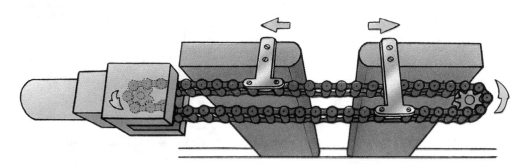

When the chain turns counterclockwise, the sliding doors open.

Automatic Teller Machine

Imagine that you keep your money in a bank, but you need to take some out to spend. When the bank is closed, you can visit an automatic teller machine (ATM). You can find these machines all over town. An ATM can give you some cash, but it's not free money! The ATM tells your bank to subtract that amount of money from your bank account.

To use an ATM, you slide your ATM card into the *card slot*. Magnetic particles on the card are read by the machine. The card tells the ATM's computer your bank's name and your bank account number.

Next, you type in your special password—your *personal identification number* (PIN). The computer reads your PIN and decides if it's the one that goes with your bank account. If it is, the computer will let you have some money. This system keeps other people from taking money out of your account, even if they have your card.

Now you type in how much money you want. If you type in $30.00, the computer signals the *cash dispenser* to pull 30 dollars' worth of bills off the stacks of money stored in the machine. Suction cups come down onto a stack of bills. A suction machine (like a vacuum cleaner) picks up the top bill on the stack and moves it aside. It

stacks up bills until the stack contains 30 dollars. Then wheels push the money out through the slot for you to pick up.

The ATM uses a *modem* (see page 127) to get information from your bank. This device links up one computer to another. The ATM checks with the bank's computer to make sure you have at least

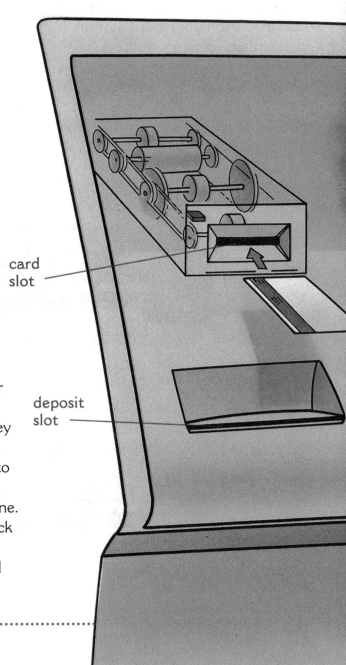

card slot

deposit slot

30 dollars in your account. If you don't, the ATM won't give you the money. Once you have taken out 30 dollars, the ATM tells the bank's computer to subtract 30 dollars from your bank account.

You can also put, or *deposit,* money into your bank account using an ATM.

You put money in an envelope and slide it into the *deposit slot.* The ATM makes a record of your deposit, and the envelope goes into a locked bin. Later, a bank worker will count the money in your envelope and add that amount to your account.

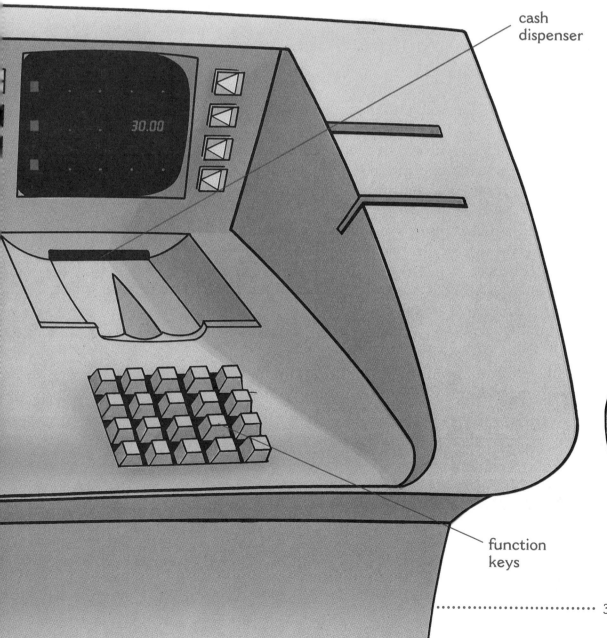

cash dispenser

function keys

In 1993, police noticed a man repeatedly pushing the buttons on an ATM and trying to get money to come out. The police arrested him and took him away. They didn't believe his story that he had mistaken the ATM for a telephone and was trying to make a long-distance call to his mother in England.

Bar Code Scanner

The error rate for bar code scanners is 1 in 100,000. The human error rate is 1 in 300. Perhaps even more important, your purchases can be totaled up to five times faster with a bar code scanner.

Each product in a store has a number. It is on the product's package. The number is a *Universal Product Code* (UPC). The UPC is made up of black stripes (bars) and white spaces. The store's computer reads these bar codes as numbers.

There are several kinds of scanners that read bar codes. Both kinds enter the name and price of the product into the cash register *automatically*—on their own. One kind of scanner looks like a space gun. The clerk aims the scanner at the code.

Another kind of scanner is built into the counter. The checker slides the package over a glass plate in the counter. The scanner sits under this glass plate. The scanner shines light from a *laser* onto mirrors. A laser is a narrow, powerful light beam. The mirrors reflect the light up through the glass plate and onto the bar code.

The white spaces between the black bars act like mirrors. They reflect the laser light back into the scanner. The bars do not reflect the light. The *detector* picks up the reflections from the white spaces and converts the pattern of light and dark into a signal, which goes to a computer.

To help the scanner read the bar code, the laser beam shines through a spinning disk. This disk makes the bar code look *three-dimensional* to the scanner. The product does not have to be held straight over the glass plate. The scanner can read the code at many angles.

The computer then changes the bar pattern into the code number for that product. Once the computer has the product's number, it "looks up" its name and price, which have already been entered into the computer's memory. The computer finds the name and price and prints them out in less than a second! The scanner beeps when the computer has picked up the code. It is then ready to read the next bar code.

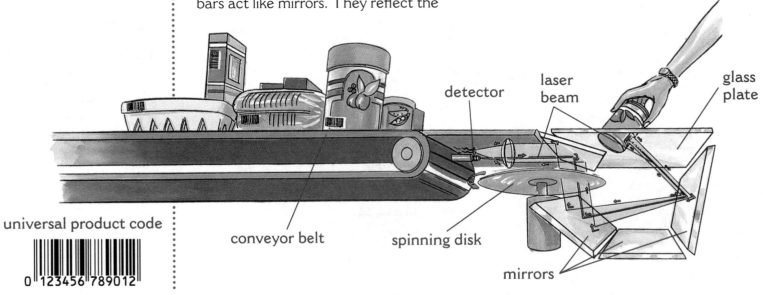

universal product code

0 123456 789012

detector

laser beam

glass plate

conveyor belt

spinning disk

mirrors

Neon Light

high voltage transformer

neon gas

glass tubing

In his science fiction book *When the Sleeper Awakes*, H.G. Wells wrote about neon signs. The book was published in 1899. Eleven years later, neon lighting was invented.

A neon light uses electricity and gas to glow. The light is made of glass tubing filled with neon gas. Electricity flows through the gas.

A *high-voltage transformer* changes standard electricity to high-voltage electricity. This high-voltage electricity excites the gas. Exciting the gas lets the electricity flow from one end of the tube to the other. As the high-voltage electricity runs through the neon gas in the tube, the gas glows.

Different gases glow different colors. Neon gas glows red. Argon gas glows blue. By coating the tubing with special powders or using colored tubing, sign makers can create many colors.

To make a neon sign, glass tubing is bent into a shape. Letters, words, and pictures can be made from the tubing.

In 1910, Georges Claude, a French scientist, created neon lighting. Claude's problem with his neon tubes was that the light they gave out was always red. It took years of experimenting to discover that putting powders in the tubing could change the color of the light.

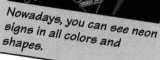

Nowadays, you can see neon signs in all colors and shapes.

Traffic Light

A traffic light changes from green to yellow to red to control the flow of traffic through an intersection. A timer controls how long each color stays lit. The traffic light for one street has to be perfectly timed with the traffic light for the cross street. Otherwise, both streets might have a green light at the same time, and cars would crash into each other!

A control box contains the timer and the switches that control both traffic lights. It usually hangs on a nearby pole. Inside the control box is a motor. It turns the *timer drum,* which is a wide wheel with *tabs* sticking out. The tabs control how long each light stays on. As the timer drum turns, the tabs move past an electrical switch. When a tab hits the switch, it turns the switch on, which makes the *cam motor* turn on for a short time.

The *cam motor gear* turns the *sector gear.* This gear doesn't have a round shape like most gears. It is shaped like a slice of pie. The cam motor gear rolls from one end of the sector gear to the other. This action pushes forward a hooked piece called a *pawl.* The pawl moves one notch ahead on the *camshaft gear.* Then the spring makes the sector gear and the pawl move back to where they started. The pawl makes the camshaft gear and the *camshaft* turn just a little bit.

Along the camshaft are notched wheels called *cams.* Each cam controls a switch. There is one switch for each of

On average, a traffic light will last 18 years before it has to be replaced.

the six lights, and an extra switch that resets the timing if the power goes out.

When the top part of the switch clicks into a notch on the cam, the switch flips down, closing the switch and turning on the light. You can see that the switches are down for the green light on Main

cam motor gear

sector gear

spring

pawl

camshaft

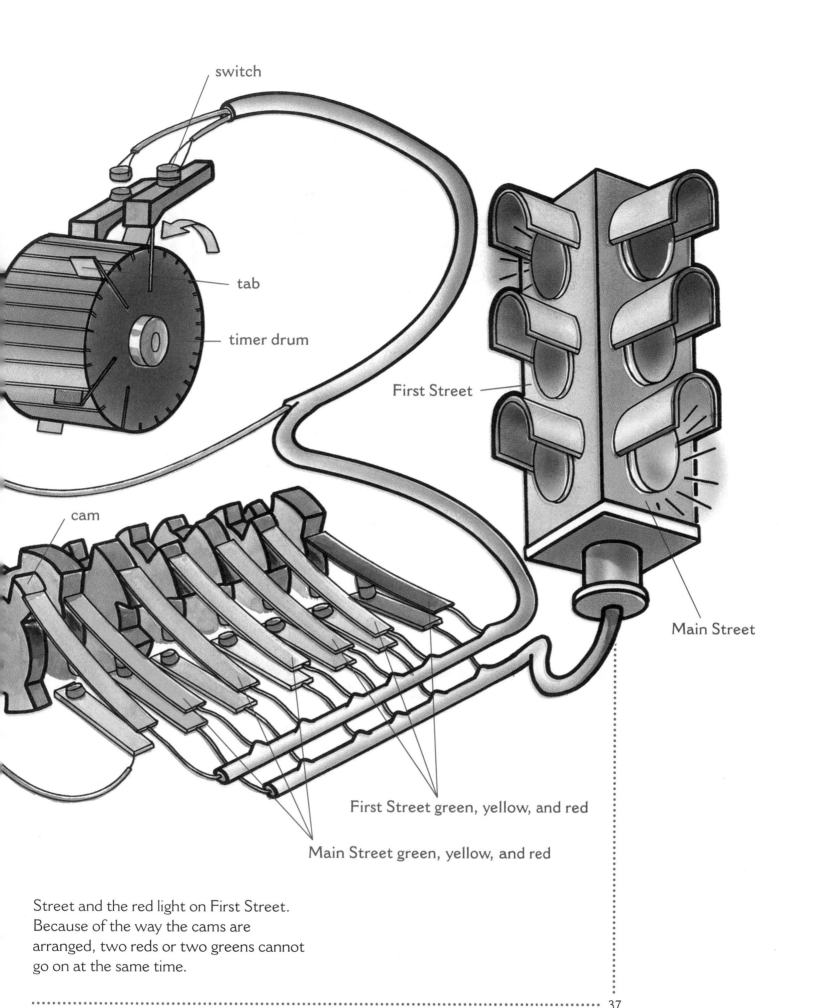

switch

tab

timer drum

cam

First Street

Main Street

First Street green, yellow, and red

Main Street green, yellow, and red

Street and the red light on First Street.
Because of the way the cams are
arranged, two reds or two greens cannot
go on at the same time.

Bridge

pier

pier

Truss bridge

A bridge can be as simple as a plank laid across a stream. Like any bridge, a simple bridge has two loads to carry: the weight of the traffic that crosses the bridge and the weight of the bridge itself.

To hold up all that weight, the bridge must have strong supports, called *piers*, at either end. The piers can't be too far apart. If they are, the bridge might sag in the middle. This problem can be solved by placing piers in the water to hold up the center of the bridge.

Suppose you need a bridge across a wide, deep river. Building lots of piers would be too difficult and expensive. Instead, you could build a *truss bridge*. The long roadway on a truss bridge is held up by a strong framework or truss which is made of triangles. Since triangles can't change shape unless one leg changes length or breaks, they keep the roadway from sagging. Together, all the triangles are lightweight but very strong.

If you wanted a bridge that big boats could cross under, you might need a *drawbridge*. The roadway on this kind of

To cross the famous Golden Gate Bridge in San Francisco, motorists have to pay a toll. If a person does not have the money, he or she can leave something equal in value to the toll. The item is tagged, and the owner can return later and pay the toll to get it back. But sometimes people don't come back. Over the years, drivers have left a can of motor oil, a tool kit, music cassettes, a set of silver tableware, a TV, men's wedding rings (these are left by the dozen), a set of false teeth, swim fins, a blouse, a frying pan, a toilet plunger, and many more items. The most expensive thing ever left was a $7,000 diamond wristwatch. Years passed, and the owner did not return for it. Finally, it was sold at auction for $5.

Golden Gate Bridge

bridge moves upward with a tilting motion, much like a teeter-totter. On one side of the "teeter-totter" is a large *counterweight* to balance the weight of the roadway. Since the roadway and the counterweight are well balanced, only a small motor is needed to raise the bridge. The motor turns *gears* (toothed wheels) that run along a *drive track,* controlling the bridge's movement.

Beside drawbridges, there are other kinds of movable bridges. *Lift bridges* have a center section between two towers. The section moves up but stays level as it moves. In *swing bridges,* part of the roadway turns sideways to clear the way for boats.

gear

drive track

Drawbridge

counterweight

Another kind of bridge for wide rivers is the *suspension bridge.* In this kind of bridge, the roadway is held up by strong wire ropes called cables. The cables hang over tall towers, with the ends of the cables connected firmly to the shore.

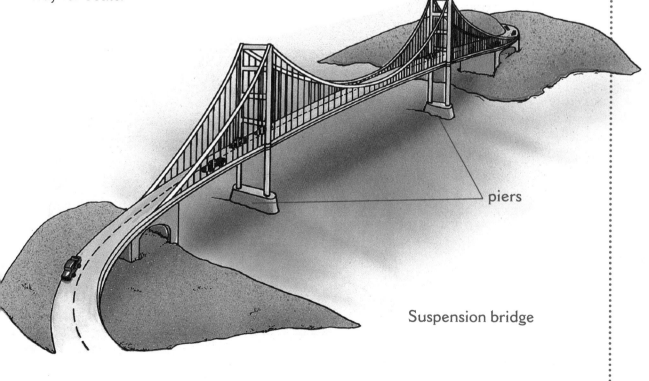

piers

Suspension bridge

Etch A Sketch Drawing Board

The Etch A Sketch may be an unusual drawing tool, but stranger things than this have been used. Artists have done their work using grease guns, nail guns, and staplers. One artist used paint made of ground-up mummies. Perhaps the strangest piece of artwork of all time was one done by John Banvard. In 1845, he completed a picture that showed scenes along the Mississippi River. Banvard's painting was on a canvas that was three miles long! It was exhibited like a giant scroll, with the canvas rolled from one huge spindle to another.

When you use an Etch A Sketch drawing board, you're actually scraping powder off a piece of glass, instead of putting lines of ink on paper.

1. The Etch A Sketch drawing board has a screen.

2. The screen is set into a box. The box is not deep. Inside the box, under the screen, is aluminum powder. The powder is like dust. Small plastic beads inside the box keep the aluminum powdery. Turning the box over and shaking it makes the beads spread the powder over the inside of the screen. When the box is turned right-side up again, a thin layer of powder sticks to the plastic. The screen looks silver.

3. Two knobs on the top of the box are connected to tiny pulleys inside the board. A pulley is a wheel with a groove. The groove holds a long string. Twisting the knobs makes the pulleys turn.

4. Loops of string pass over each pulley.

5. Each of the loops of string is connected to a rod. The left knob moves a rod that runs from the top to the bottom of the drawing board. The right knob moves a rod that runs from side to side. The two rods cross each other.

6. At the place where the two rods cross is a sliding plastic point. The plastic point presses against the inside of the glass screen.

7. When the left knob turns, the plastic point moves left and right across the screen. When the right knob turns, the plastic point moves up and down the screen.

Wherever the plastic point goes, it rubs the aluminum powder from the inside of the screen. Where the powder is rubbed off, you can see through the glass. Because the inside of the box is dark, the lines show up as dark lines on the silver screen.

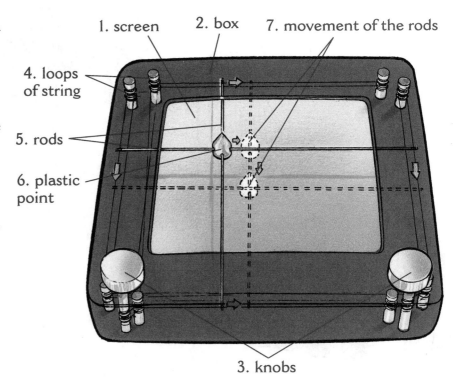

1. screen 2. box 7. movement of the rods
4. loops of string
5. rods
6. plastic point
3. knobs

Frisbee Flying Disk

A nything flat will fly for a short distance—as long as it is thrown so that it spins. The spinning makes the object act like a *gyroscope*. A gyroscope will keep spinning in the same direction until *friction* stops it. This is called gyroscopic force. Friction is created when two things rub against each other. Friction slows moving objects down.

To throw a Frisbee flying disk, you toss it forward with a spin. Gyroscopic force keeps it pointing in the same direction you threw it. Throw a Frisbee straight and it flies straight. Throw it at an angle and it keeps flying at the same angle—as long as it has speed. Gyroscopic force will keep the Frisbee spinning at this angle until gravity and friction make it fall.

Because of its special shape, a Frisbee flying disk flies farther than does a plain, flat disk. A Frisbee's top is curved and the bottom is hollow. The air passing over the top is spread out over the larger, curved area. The pressure of the air passing over the top is less than the pressure of the air passing under the bottom. The difference in pressure pushes the Frisbee up. This is *lift*. When the Frisbee starts out, its lift is strong. As the Frisbee slows down, its lift gets weak.

Believe it or not, the Frisbee flying disk is named after the Frisbie Pie Company, a Connecticut bakery that was in business back in 1900. For fun, people tossed around empty pie tins, which had the name "Frisbie Bakery" on the bottom. In the early 1950s, a man named W. Morrison invented a metal tossing toy he called the "Flyin' Saucer." Because metal could be dangerous, he soon switched to plastic. Then he changed the name. Morrison, who was living in California at the time, recalled his younger days in Connecticut where he and his friends had tossed around pie tins from the local bakery, and decided to name his invention the "Frisbee."

Remote-Controlled Toy

Radio waves can carry more than just sound. Remote-controlled toys use radio waves to carry signals from the controls to the toy. These signals make the toy move.

Inside the control is a *transmitter.* The transmitter sends a signal through the control's antenna. ("Transmit" means "to send.") An antenna on the toy picks up the signal and carries it to the toy's radio *receiver.* The signal switches the toy's motor on or off. The control and the toy must be close enough for the signals to reach the toy.

A toy car needs more than just a few signals. It can do more than just stop and go. A remote-controlled car can steer, speed up, and slow down.

On a toy car, a motor is used for each type of control. These motors are *reversible.* They can go opposite ways—fast or slow, right or left, backward or

forward. The control panel has a lever for each motor. (Some controls use buttons, joysticks, or small steering wheels.) This prevents the signals for forward and backward movement from getting mixed up with the signals for left and right turns.

Once these signals reach the radio receiver, the receiver sends an electric signal to a motor. The receiver has wires that connect to one or more electric motors. The motors turn gears in the car. A gear is a wheel with teeth.

One signal travels through the wire that is attached to the *drive motor.* The

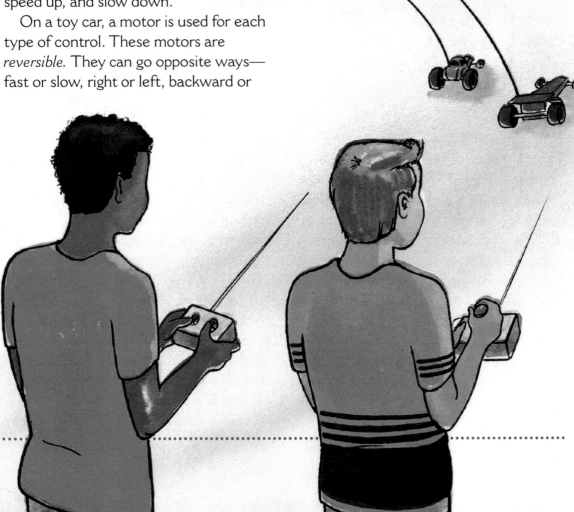

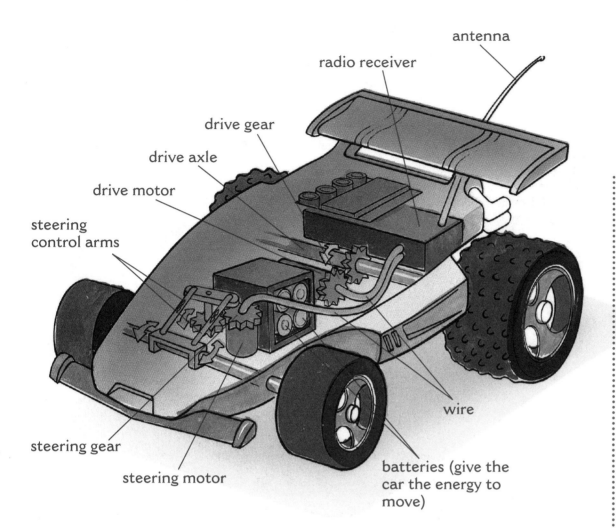

antenna

radio receiver

drive gear

drive axle

drive motor

steering control arms

steering gear

steering motor

wire

batteries (give the car the energy to move)

drive motor turns the *drive gear*. As the drive gear turns, it turns another gear. This other gear is attached to the *drive axle*. An axle is a metal rod with wheels at each end. The drive motor makes the car go fast or slow.

Another signal travels through the wire that is attached to the steering motor. The *steering motor* turns the steering gear. As the *steering gear* turns, it turns the gear that is attached to the *steering control arms*. The steering control arms make the car go left or right.

Some control systems are different. Pressing a button, for example, might change the direction of the motor. Letting up on a button and pressing it again might swing the car out of a right turn and into a left turn.

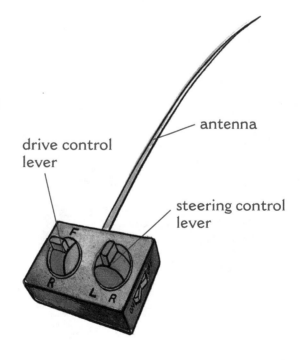

drive control lever

antenna

steering control lever

During World Wars I and II, the Germans developed remote-controlled boats, planes, and miniature tanks. These were not toys—they were packed with bombs. Remote controls guided the vehicles toward the enemy. When they reached their target, the bombs were exploded. The idea for remote-controlled toys came from these weapons of war during the early 1950s.

Windup Toy

What makes a windup toy move? A windup toy uses a *spring* to store and release the energy that makes it work. (A spring is a thin, curled piece of metal.) When a spring is wound up, it stores energy. As the spring unwinds, it *releases,* or gives off, energy. Energy makes things move. The tighter the spring is wound, the more energy it stores.

Turning the toy's *key* winds the *mainspring*. As the mainspring is wound, a *pawl* catches in the teeth of the *ratchet wheel*. The ratchet wheel is a *gear,* a wheel with teeth. The pawl lets the ratchet wheel move in only one direction. The pawl and ratchet wheel keep the mainspring from unwinding right away. One end of the spring is fixed to the toy. The other end of the spring is fixed to the key.

Letting go of the key lets the mainspring unwind. The pawl does not hold back the ratchet wheel. The pawl

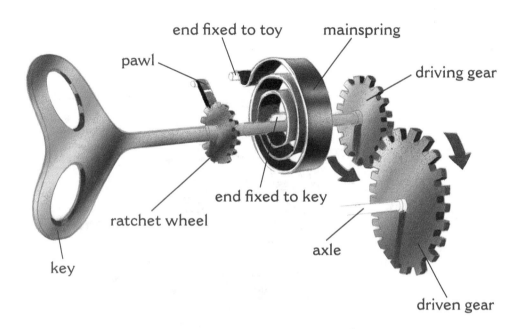

pawl

end fixed to toy

mainspring

driving gear

key

ratchet wheel

end fixed to key

axle

driven gear

clicks over the teeth of the ratchet wheel as the key turns. As the mainspring unwinds, it moves a system of gears. The gears make the toy's parts move.

In a windup toy car, for example, two gears make the car's wheels turn. One gear—the *driving gear*—is attached to the key. The other gear—the *driven*

gear—is attached to the *axle*. An axle is a rod with a wheel at each end. The teeth of the driving gear fit into the teeth of the driven gear.

As the spring unwinds, energy moves from the spring into the driving gear. The driving gear then turns the driven gear, the driven gear turns the axle, and the axle turns the wheels. The energy from the mainspring keeps the gears turning into each other and the wheels moving.

Windup toys were invented in Germany during the Middle Ages. The very first may have been a toy train that went around a circular track. To operate it, a top was stuck into a gear beside the track. The top was then wound up and began spinning. As it spun, the train went around and around.

Water Pistol

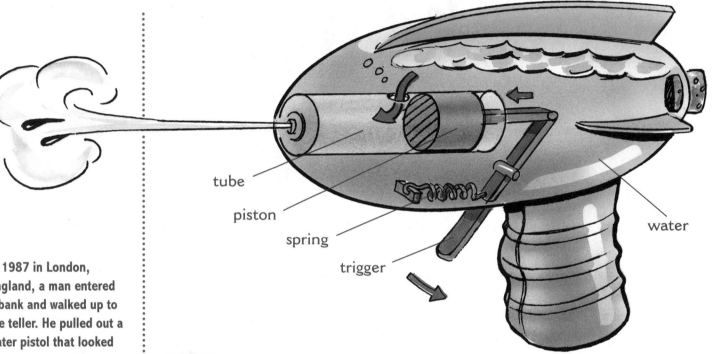

tube

piston

spring

trigger

water

A water pistol squirts because water can't be squeezed to fit into a smaller space. Try it yourself: Fill a balloon with water and squeeze it. Watch what the water does. It shifts from end to end, but it doesn't get smaller.

Inside a water pistol is water and a tube. The tube has a tiny hole in the end. A *piston* fits inside the tube. A piston is a plug that slides back and forth. A spring connects the piston and the trigger. Squeezing the trigger pushes the piston forward. The piston moves toward the hole. Letting go of the trigger moves the piston back.

The tube has another hole in the top. This hole lets water into the tube when the piston is pulled back. Squeeze the trigger and the piston pushes the water through the hole in the end of the tube, straight out of the pistol. The water has only one place to go—it must go out.

The piston is many times bigger than the little hole in the end of the pistol. When the piston pushes forward, the water must go through the hole much faster than the piston is pushing. The high speed makes a hard, thin stream of water. The water pistol squirts!

Other kinds of squirt guns work in different ways. Some use a pump to build up air pressure in the squirt gun. When you squeeze the trigger, the air forces the water out. These pistols are often big and hold a lot of water. Some water pistols even have lights and sound effects. These pistols look and sound like space guns.

Soap Bubbles

Bubbles can be made from soapy water because the soap allows the water to make a stretchy film. Water is made of *molecules*. A molecule is a particle that is so tiny, it is invisible to the eye. Plain water molecules hold together very tightly. They produce *surface tension* in the water, which means that the outer layer of molecules, on the surface, acts like a skin. A drop of water hangs on the edge of a faucet because of surface tension. The molecules of the water stick together to keep the drop from breaking. A small insect can walk across the water because of surface tension. The surface tension is strong enough to carry the insect's weight.

You can't blow bubbles with plain water. The surface tension of water is too strong—the molecules will not stretch far from each other. Soap or detergent makes the surface tension less strong. It lets the skin stretch. Too little soap will not let the skin stretch enough. Too much soap lets the skin stretch too much. Just the right amount of soap in water will let you make bubbles.

A bubble wand is a favorite way to make bubbles. Dipping the wand into the soapy water coats the loop with soap. Blowing air into the circle or waving the wand fills the film of soap with air. The pocket of air grows until the end of the stretchy film shuts. A bubble is born!

Most of the time, bubbles are round. A round shape stretches the skin evenly in all directions.

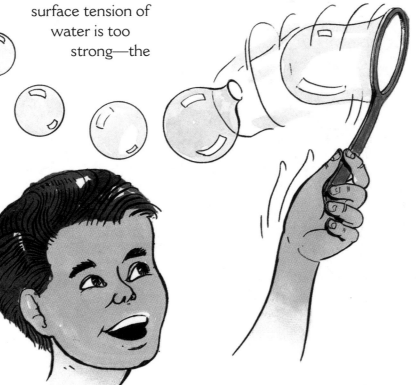

One of the most interesting uses of bubbles is in helping scientists study atomic particles. Scientists shoot the particles through what is called a "bubble chamber." Though the particles are too small to be seen, they leave strings of tiny bubbles called "tracks." By studying these tracks, scientists can learn much about the atom.

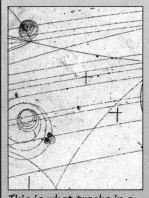

This is what tracks in a bubble chamber look like.

Yo-yo

Throwing the yo-yo down—with your finger looped through one end of the string—starts the yo-yo spinning. The spinning makes the yo-yo act like a *gyroscope*. A gyroscope spins in the same direction until *friction* slows it down. Friction is the resistance to motion created when two objects rub against each other or an object rubs against the air. If you slide a book across a table, friction is what slows the book down. The *gyrating* action keeps the yo-yo from twisting the string.

The string is tied around the *axle*. The axle is the short, smooth rod that connects the two disks of the yo-yo. Friction keeps the axle from slipping away from the string. If the string is wound tightly around the axle, the yo-yo comes back up as it reaches the end of the string. Friction between the string and the axle makes the yo-yo return.

If the string is not wound tightly around the axle, the yo-yo keeps on spinning at the end of the string. There is not enough friction between the string and the axle to cause the yo-yo to climb back up the string. The axle slips around inside the loop of string. Tugging on the string creates enough friction to make the yo-yo climb back up the string.

The yo-yo was originally a hunting weapon used in the Philippine Islands. It was made of a large disk of wood or stone with twine wrapped around it. A hunter would throw the weapon, and the twine would snare an animal by the legs. In the 1920s, an enterprising American named Donald Duncan visited the Philippines. There, he saw a hunter using a yo-yo. Duncan made the yo-yo smaller and transformed it into a toy. Soon he was selling yo-yos in the United States by the thousands.

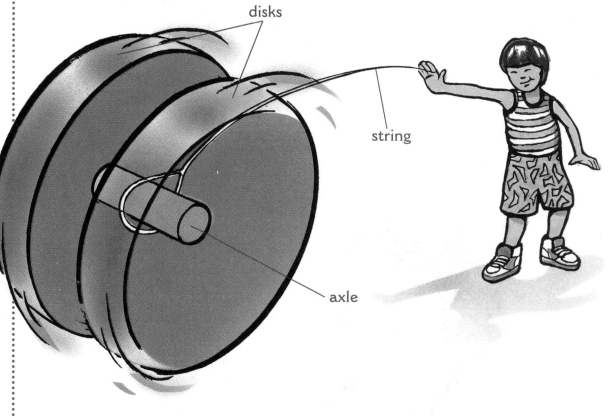

disks

string

axle

Top

A top will stay up on its point as long as it is spinning fast enough. A top acts like a *gyroscope*. A gyroscope will keep spinning at the same speed and in the same direction until *friction* stops it. Friction, created when two objects rub against each other, slows moving objects down. Friction is made at the point where the top touches the ground and by the air that the top moves through. As friction slows its spinning speed, the top leans. It wobbles. It makes bigger—and slower—circles. At last, the top falls down.

Some toy tops are made to spin with a pull of a tightly wound string. Other toy tops are made to spin by pumping a handle.

In a pump-handle top, the handle sticks out from the center of the top. A groove cuts into the handle. The groove makes a spiral along the length of the rod. A metal plate inside the top fits into the groove. A downward push on the handle forces the plate along the spiral, which makes the top turn. A spring pops the handle up, and the top spins.

spiral-grooved rod

metal plate

spring

Pump-handle top

String top

Clay tops were spun by Egyptian and Babylonian children as early as 3000 B.C. Historians are sure the tops were toys because they were discovered in children's graves along with sets of marbles.

Boomerang

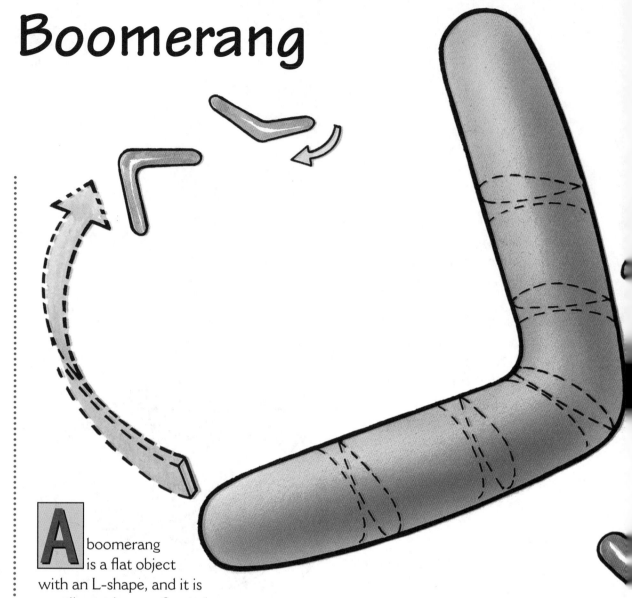

A boomerang is a flat object with an L-shape, and it is usually made out of wood. When you throw a boomerang, it flies through the air. If the boomerang has been made just right, it will come back to you when you throw it. Boomerangs are used for fun or sport. Native Australians and others used the boomerang as a weapon or tool.

A boomerang that returns can do so because of the shape of its two arms and because it spins. Each arm is shaped like the wing of a plane, with one rounded edge, called the *leading edge,* and one sharper edge, called the *trailing edge.* The leading edge of one arm faces toward the inside of the L-shape. The leading edge of the other arm faces toward the outside.

To throw a boomerang, you hold it so that one flat end is against your hand. Then, you lift the boomerang behind your head and throw it as if you were chopping down through the air. The boomerang turns over and over in its flight. Both leading edges cut through the air as the boomerang spins.

The arms of a boomerang act like the wings of an airplane. When air flows over an airplane wing, the air moves faster over the curved top of the wing than over the flat bottom side. This faster movement creates *lift,* a force that moves the wing up. (See page 162.) The air flows over the arms of the

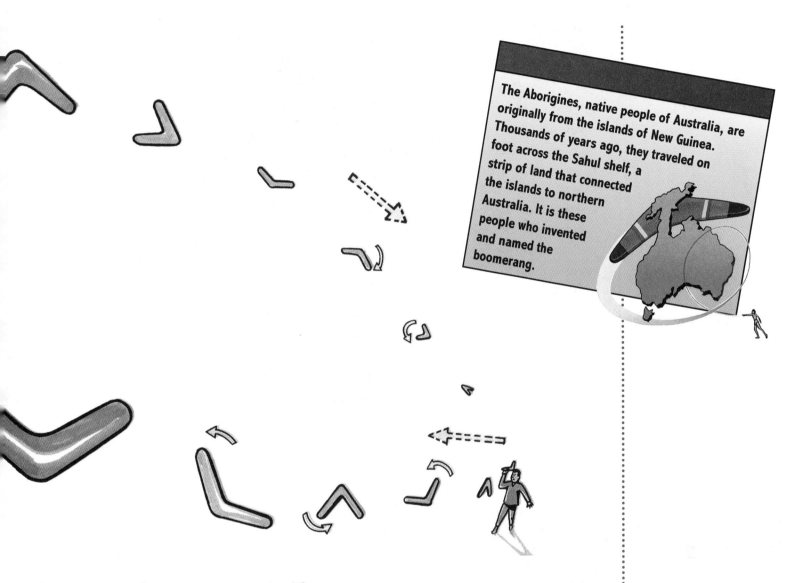

The Aborigines, native people of Australia, are originally from the islands of New Guinea. Thousands of years ago, they traveled on foot across the Sahul shelf, a strip of land that connected the islands to northern Australia. It is these people who invented and named the boomerang.

boomerang in the same way, creating lift. But the boomerang doesn't go up because of the way it is tilted on its edge when it is thrown. The lift keeps the boomerang at the same height above the ground as it starts to travel in a large circle.

Both arms create lift, but the lift on the upper arm is greater. Lift depends on speed, and the upper arm moves faster than the lower arm. The upper arm moves forward at the speed of the boomerang *plus* the speed that it is turning. The lower arm moves forward at the speed of the boomerang *minus* the turning speed, since the lower arm is moving back. The difference in lift and the spinning make the boomerang travel in a large circle. Back it comes, ready for you to catch it!

Teeter-totter

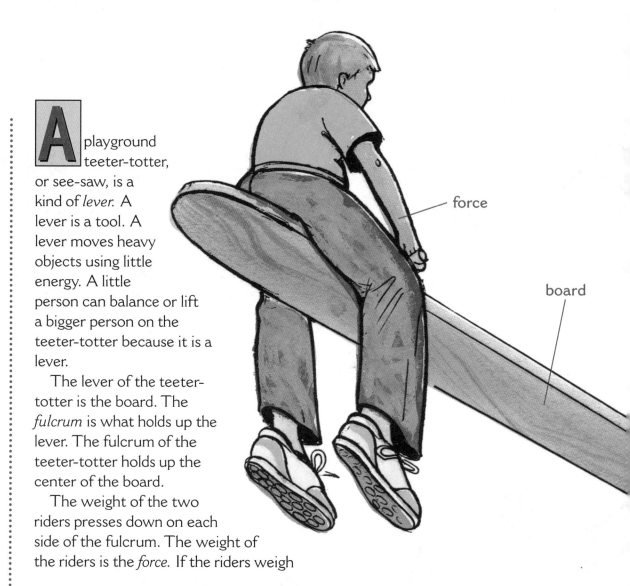

force

board

A playground teeter-totter, or see-saw, is a kind of *lever*. A lever is a tool. A lever moves heavy objects using little energy. A little person can balance or lift a bigger person on the teeter-totter because it is a lever.

The lever of the teeter-totter is the board. The *fulcrum* is what holds up the lever. The fulcrum of the teeter-totter holds up the center of the board.

The weight of the two riders presses down on each side of the fulcrum. The weight of the riders is the *force*. If the riders weigh

One of the strangest uses of the teeter-totter was in the Coliseum in ancient Rome. In one act, two clowns were put in baskets. One basket was put on each end of a teeter-totter. Then a lion was set free in the ring. When it came after one of the clowns, the clown would push off—and up—into the air. Then the animal would run toward the basket on the ground. And that clown would suddenly go up out of reach. Up and down the clowns would go. The ancient Romans thought this was funny. It seems they had a rather cruel sense of humor!

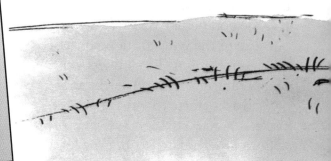

the same—and sit the same distance away from the fulcrum—the force is equal. The board balances. This can be figured out with multiplication. First multiply the force on one side and its distance to the fulcrum. Then multiply the force on the other side and its distance to the fulcrum. If both sides are equal, the board balances.

If the riders do not weigh the same, the force is not equal. The board does not balance. The bigger person sinks to the ground.

To balance the board, the force must be evened out. There are two ways to even out the force. The fulcrum can be moved closer to the bigger person, or the bigger person can move toward the fulcrum.

Let's take an example. One rider weighs 100 pounds and another rider weighs 50 pounds. The 100-pound rider must sit twice as close to the fulcrum as the 50-pound rider. (This is because 100 pounds is twice as heavy as 50 pounds.)

By keeping the teeter-totter balanced between the two riders, they will both be able to push off the ground in turn. They will "teeter" on the fulcrum.

fulcrum

Roller Coaster

3. hills

4. loop

Roller coasters work because of *gravity* and *stored energy.* Gravity is the force that pulls us to Earth. Without gravity, we would float up into the air.

1. When the roller coaster car moves, stored energy is changed into energy that is used.

2. The safety bars are lowered into place and the ride begins. A chain under the tracks pulls the train of cars to the top of the *chain-driven hill.* A roller coaster may have one or more chain-driven hills. The chain-driven hills are higher than the hills in between. The roller coaster cars store energy as they are being pulled up the hill. Gravity pulls the cars down the hill. The cars have enough energy to keep rolling up the next hill.

3. The other hills of a roller coaster cannot be higher than the chain-driven ones. Not enough energy is stored in the roller coaster cars to climb that high again. Each hill the cars climb uses more energy than can be stored in the next run down the hill.

4. Going around a loop makes a roller coaster car turn upside-down. The cars of a roller coaster would keep moving in a straight line if there were no tracks. The tracks make the cars go around in a circle. The speed of the car when it is forced to make the loop creates a force that prevents the car and you from falling. You don't fall out when the roller coaster makes a loop.

5. The cars of a loop roller coaster have wheels that touch the top, side, and

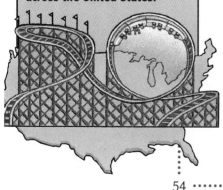

Disc jockey Jim King holds the world record for nonstop roller coaster riding. In 1980, King rode a roller coaster for over 15 days and nights, making 6,950 laps. On the ride, he covered 3,475 miles. That's the same distance as a trip across the United States!

2. chain-driven hill

1. roller coaster car

5. wheels

bottom of the track. These extra wheels make sure the cars stay on the track. Side wheels keep the car from slipping sideways. Bottom wheels hold the upside-down car onto the track.

At the end of the ride, there are no chain-driven hills to give the cars more energy to move. *Friction* slows the cars down. Friction is created when objects rub against one another or an object rubs against the air. The operator stops the slow-moving cars with the brakes.

Bumper Car

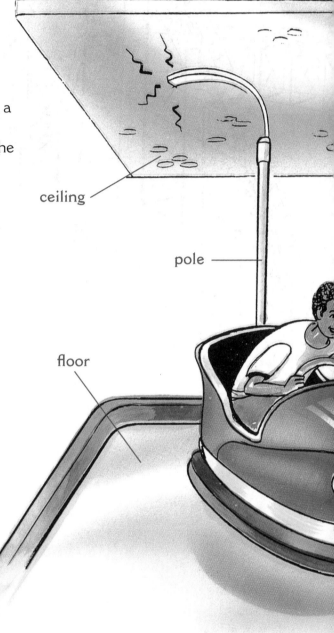

ceiling

pole

floor

Electricity, not gasoline, makes bumper cars go. Electricity travels in a *circuit*. A circuit is a loop. In a bumper car, the electrical circuit has three parts. The parts are the ceiling, the tall pole on the car, and the floor.

A metal net hangs from the ceiling. The car's pole touches the net all the time. The car's metal wheels touch the floor all the time, too. Electricity flows from the ceiling and through the pole. From the pole, electricity goes through the car's motor and into the wheels. From the wheels, electricity goes into the floor. Then it flows back up to the ceiling the same way. The circuit is complete.

Electricity drives the motor that makes the bumper car's wheels turn. Turning wheels make the bumper car move across the floor.

Once you are safely seated in a bumper car, the operator starts the ride. The ride operator starts the flow of electricity by flipping a switch. By pressing the foot pedals, you control how much electricity goes to the car's motor. Pressing hard sends more electricity to the motor. The car speeds up. Pressing softly makes the car go slower.

Bumper cars are built to bump other cars. You can go fast or slow, and you can steer—but you can't back up. A bumper car has wheels that turn all the way to the side. Turning the wheels to the side lets you "spin out" of a crash.

Pads inside the car and on the steering wheel keep you from getting hurt. Some cars have shoulder straps. The straps keep you from being thrown forward in a crash. The outside edge of the bumper car has rubber bumpers. They make the bumps less rough.

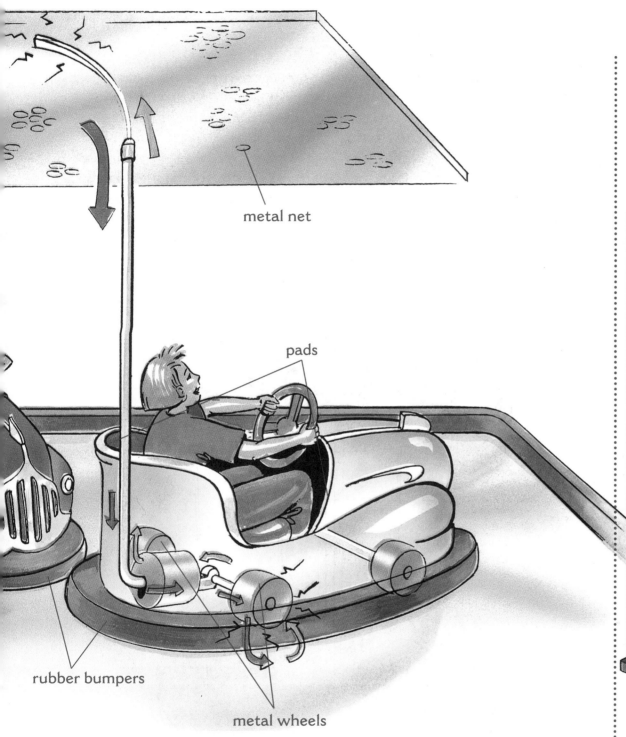

metal net

pads

rubber bumpers

metal wheels

Mary Channing, of Denver, Colorado, had not seen her stepsister Angie in 11 years. The two had been separated since they were nine years old, when their parents were divorced. Mary did not even know where Angie was living. Then, when Mary was on a vacation in Las Vegas, she and Angie bumped into each other—while on a bumper car ride!

FUN FUN FUN

Carousel

Nearly all carousels (or merry-go-rounds) run on electricity. At the top and in the center of a carousel is a *shaft*. The shaft is a tall pole that turns. A powerful electric motor turns the shaft. The motor starts and stops the ride and makes it go fast or slow.

A strong ring hangs from the top of the shaft. Steel *cables* connect the ring to the shaft. (A cable is a thick wire.) A circular platform hangs by steel *platform rods* from the ring overhead.

Under the *canopy* of the carousel, *cranks* stick out of the shaft. Poles are fixed to each crank, and animals are attached to the poles. More than one pole can be attached to a crank.

The carousel probably started out as a tool to train the king's knights in the Middle Ages. A knight-in-training would ride a wooden horse while trying to hit a small target with the tip of his spear. Over the years the target was changed to a brass ring. In the past, catching the brass ring on a carousel won the rider a free ride.

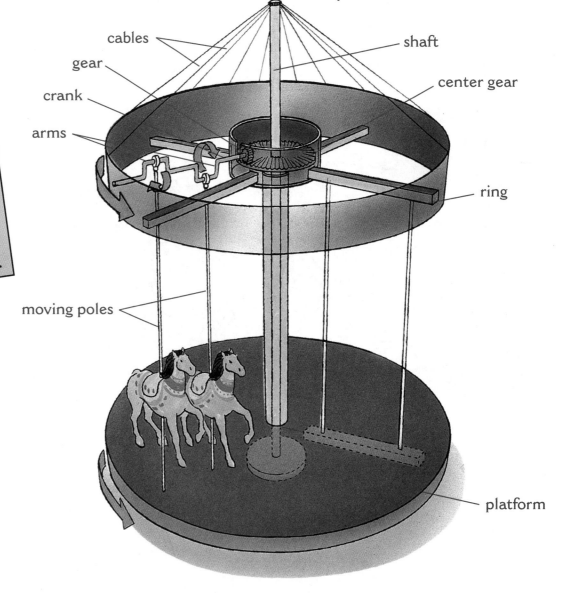

cables

gear

crank

arms

shaft

center gear

ring

moving poles

platform

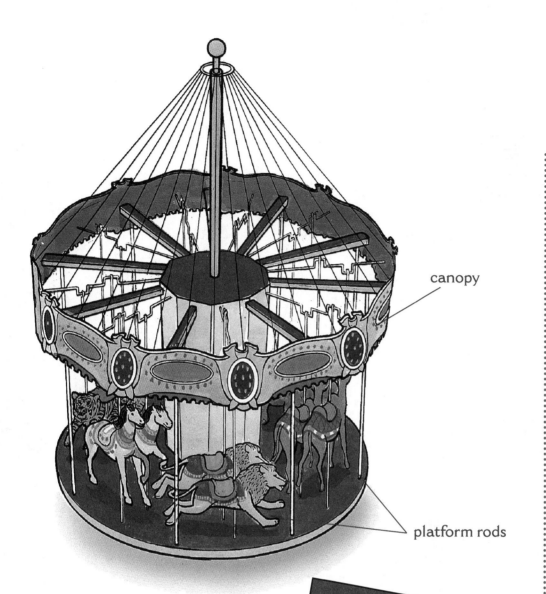

canopy

platform rods

Each pole is attached to its own arm on the crank. The *crank arm* is a U-shaped part of the crank.

Each crank has a *gear* on the end. (A gear is a wheel with teeth.) The gears meet in the center of the carousel. The teeth of the gears from the cranks fit with the teeth of the shaft's center gear. As the center gear turns around, it turns the gears on the ends of the cranks.

The motor turns the platform and the gears turn the cranks. Because each animal is attached to its own crank arm, it goes up and down as the crank turns.

The world's largest carousel is the Columbia, located in Santa Clara, California. The double-decker carousel is ten stories high and 27½ feet in circumference. It can carry 115 passengers. For the riders there are 103 carousel animals, including 52 horses, a giraffe, a camel, a lion, a tiger, a dragon, a deer, a sea horse, two ostriches, and several pigs, cats, and rabbits, plus two chariots. The cost of construction was $1.8 million.

The Columbia

Bobsled

Bobsleds are fast sleds used for racing. Some bobsleds hold two people, and others hold four. A bobsled is not much different from a plain runner sled, except that it has better controls, and it is made from special materials.

The bobsled runs on a concrete track coated with ice. To keep the ice frozen solid, the track has *refrigeration pipes.* They work the same way as the pipes in your refrigerator (see page 10). With this system, the ice can stay frozen, even if the air is 70 degrees Fahrenheit! The track curves up on the sides, because the bobsled rides up the edges on turns.

The bobsled has a place for the riders to sit and a sleek cover to help the sled cut through the air. The bobsled is made of strong, lightweight metals and plastics to keep it as light as possible. However, adding weight in the right places helps the bobsled run better. With a light sled, the riders can add weight wherever they need it to make the sled run just as fast as it can.

The riders get started by pushing the sled until it has enough speed, and then jumping in. Then, the riders must steer the sled and control its speed.

Underneath the bobsled are the *runners.* The front runners are attached to each other by a bar, and the bar connects to the sled by an upright center post. The driver can steer the sled with the front runners by pulling on cords attached to the runners. The runner bar turns on the center post. A pull on the cord on the right makes the runners and the sled turn to the right. The sled is also controlled by the riders shifting their weight around during the run.

The rider in the back uses the brake to slow down for turns and to stop. Pulling up on the brake lever makes a metal piece with sharp teeth dig into the ice.

refrigeration pipes

ice

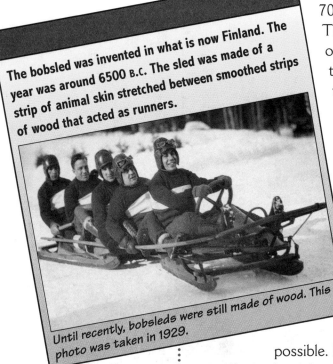

The bobsled was invented in what is now Finland. The year was around 6500 B.C. The sled was made of a strip of animal skin stretched between smoothed strips of wood that acted as runners.

Until recently, bobsleds were still made of wood. This photo was taken in 1929.

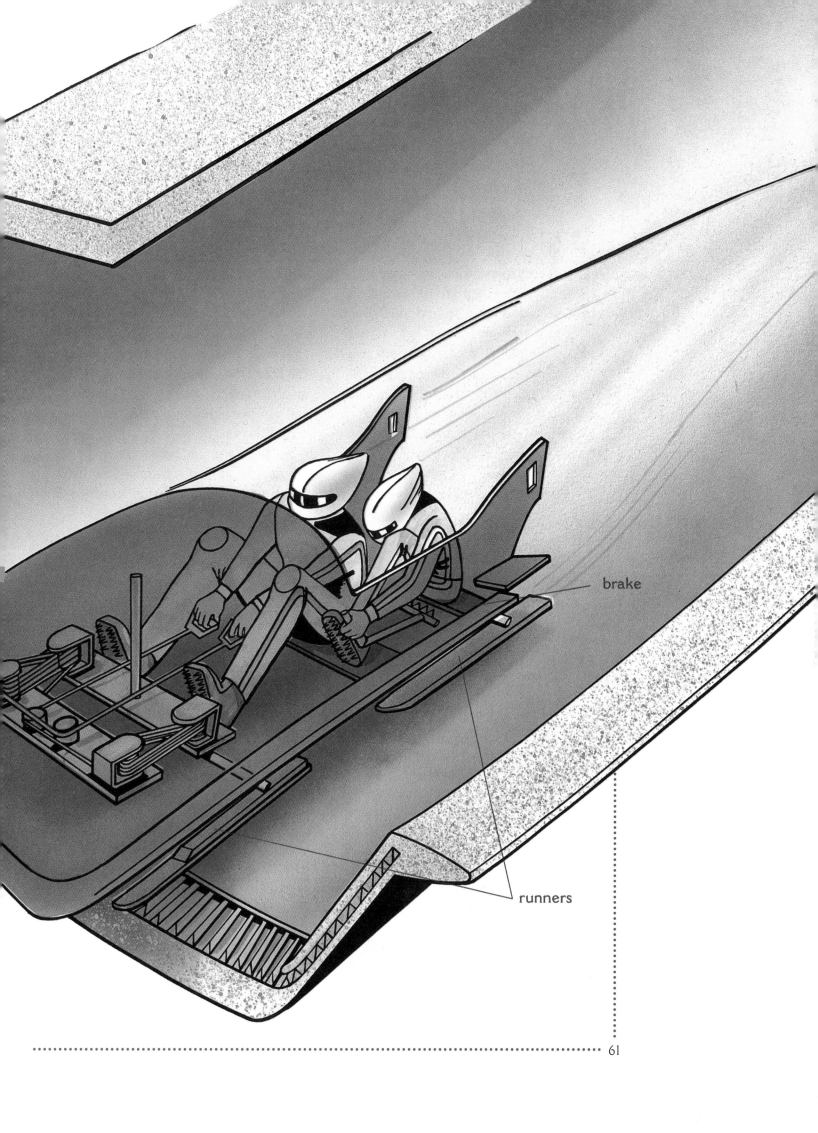

brake

runners

Magic Tricks

Most magic tricks work by *misdirection*. When you are misdirected, the magician draws your attention away from what he or she is really doing while the trick is performed. For example, when a magician pulls a rabbit out of a hat, the magician waves the wand. We are watching the wand instead of noticing that the assistant is putting a rabbit into the hat!

Magic tricks also work because people see what they expect to see—whether it is there or not. Would you ever think to count the fingers on a magician's hands? We see ten fingers because we expect to see ten fingers. A place for a magician to hide a silk scarf is a hollow fake finger. If the magician does not draw our attention to the extra finger, we never see it! Presto! A scarf is magically pulled out of the air!

A favorite magic trick is sawing a person in half. The magician and the assistant perform this trick together. The

What you see

large box

metal sheets

holes

table

box halves

What really happens

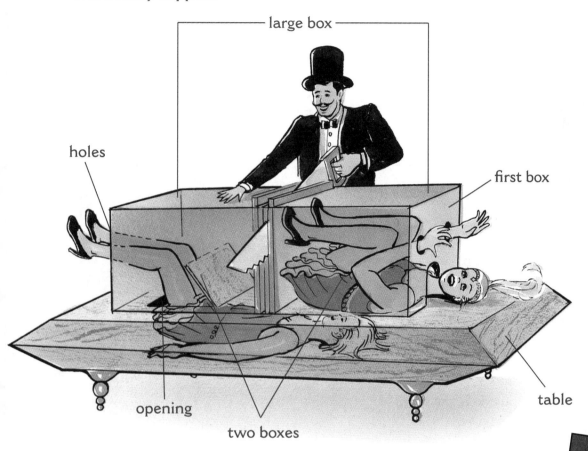

large box

holes

first box

opening

two boxes

table

assistant first climbs into a large box that is resting on a table. The box has holes at each end. One end has holes for the assistant's head and hands. The other end has holes for the assistant's feet.

The magician then saws the box—and the assistant—in half. When the magician finishes sawing, two metal sheets are slipped between the two halves of the box. The halves of the box are pushed apart. The assistant is cut in half!

The magician pushes the two halves together again and takes out the metal sheets. The assistant climbs out in one piece! Is it magic?

It is not magic. The trick works because we expect the feet, head, and hands to belong to one assistant. Actually, two assistants help the magician do this trick.

One assistant climbs into the large box. The other assistant hides inside the hollow table. The large box is really two boxes in one. The upper box is the one the assistant climbs into. The assistant curls up to keep his or her legs in the upper box. The lower box is for the hidden assistant. The hidden assistant's legs and feet go up into this box through a trapdoor in the table, and stick out of the holes on the end. It looks as if the assistant you saw climbing into the box is the one whose feet are sticking through the holes.

The saw never touches either assistant. The sheets of metal hide the fact that the large box is really two smaller boxes.

Harry Houdini was the most famous magician of all time. He was especially known for his amazing escapes. He escaped from countless jails and prisons, usually after being searched by policemen and doctors to show he had "nothing up his sleeve." He escaped from crates, bags, barrels, and coffins, usually shedding locks and chains in the process. Nobody has ever matched the feats of the great Houdini.

Magic Tricks

The disappearing scarf is another popular magic trick. The magician stuffs the scarf into either hand. The magician opens both hands and they are empty!

A magician can make a scarf disappear by using a *pull*. A pull is a small cup attached to a long, strong rubber band. The other end of the rubber band is attached to the back of the magician's belt. The cup is pulled around and tucked into the magician's belt at the side. The magician's cape hides the pull.

While the audience is listening to the magician talk and watching the magician's arms wave, the magician takes the cup in one hand. The audience does not know it is there.

The magician stuffs the scarf into the cup hidden in the hand. The magician lets go of the cup and the rubber band pulls it around. While the audience is listening to the magician's magic words and watching the magician's hands, the cup—stuffed with the scarf—zips behind the magician.

pull

cape

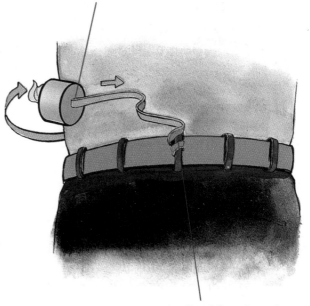

end of rubber band attached to cup

end of rubber band attached to belt

Aquarium

Fish, like people and land animals, need oxygen. They take it from the water. Lakes and oceans have plenty of water—and oxygen—to go around. In an aquarium, new oxygen must replace the used oxygen.

1. Aquariums put oxygen back into the water with an air pump. A common air pump is a belt-driven piston pump.

2. In this kind of pump, an electric motor makes the belt move.

3. The belt loops around a *pulley*. A pulley is a wheel with a groove in its center. The belt rides in the groove.

4. As the belt turns the pulley, the pulley pushes and pulls the piston. A *piston* is a rod that slides back and forth in a cylinder.

1. air pump

5. When the piston pulls back, it sucks air through an *intake valve*—a small tube through which air flows. When the piston pushes forward, the air is forced out through tubing into the aquarium's filter. The cylinder's intake valve is a one-way valve. It lets air in, but it doesn't let it out. Another one-way valve at the end of the air hose lets the air out, but will not let water in.

6. The tubing leads to the aquarium's filter. Air from the tubing pushes water from the aquarium through the filter. The filter cleans the water. Then the air flows out of the filter. The air bubbles float to the top of the tank. Some of the oxygen dissolves—or mixes into—the water. The fish have oxygen, which they take in through their gills.

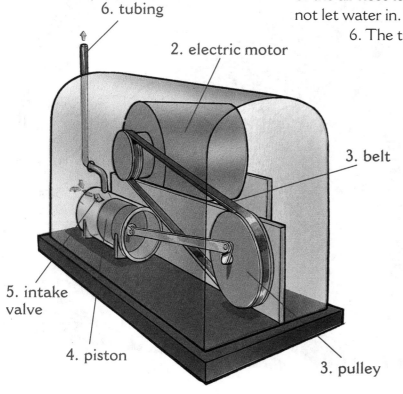

6. tubing

2. electric motor

3. belt

5. intake valve

4. piston

3. pulley

During the 1970s, a shoe company came up with one of the strangest products ever. It sounds unbelievable, but they started selling what they called Aquarium Shoes. The heels of the custom-made shoes were made of clear, hollowed-out plastic. The heels were then filled with water and live goldfish. Then off went the shoe buyer, wearing goofy fish-tank footwear.

Light Show

The basic tools for stage lighting are the *floodlight* and the *spotlight*. "Floods" have wide beams that spread over a large area. "Spots" have narrow beams that light up just one person or object. Floods and spots both give off white light. They can give off colored light when *gels* are used. Gels are pieces of clear, colored plastic that are placed over the lights.

At a concert, the lights are controlled by a computer. The computer is connected to the music's sound system. The lights can be made to flash and change in time with the music. A fog

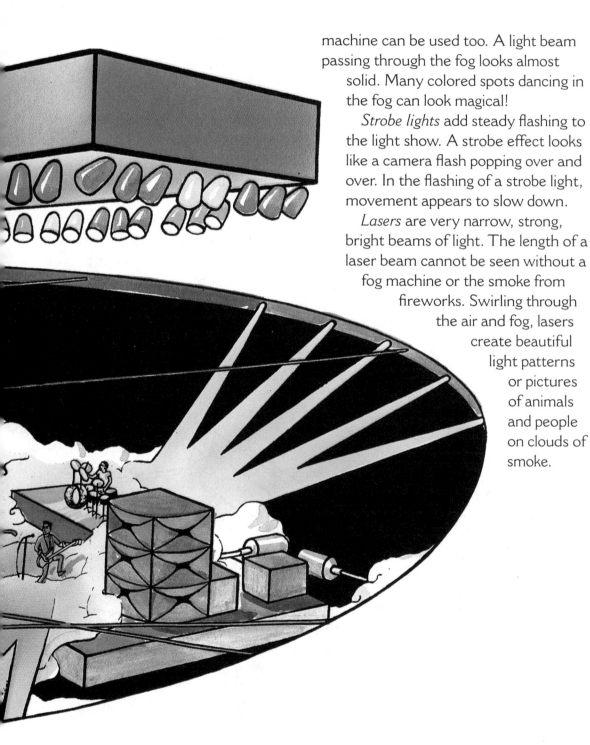

machine can be used too. A light beam passing through the fog looks almost solid. Many colored spots dancing in the fog can look magical!

Strobe lights add steady flashing to the light show. A strobe effect looks like a camera flash popping over and over. In the flashing of a strobe light, movement appears to slow down.

Lasers are very narrow, strong, bright beams of light. The length of a laser beam cannot be seen without a fog machine or the smoke from fireworks. Swirling through the air and fog, lasers create beautiful light patterns or pictures of animals and people on clouds of smoke.

The world's first light show was an advertising gimmick. One evening in 1952, the people of Paris, France, looked up to see the most unusual ad ever. On low, overhanging clouds, the name of an airline suddenly appeared in gigantic, brilliant letters. The feat was accomplished by using a complicated system of spotlights and huge color transparencies. Citizens were fascinated by what they called "skylighting" and hoped to see more in the future. The city council, however, was not impressed. It passed a law against the "projecting of lights on the clouds."

Camera and Film

A camera makes pictures (photographs) on *film*. Film is a thin sheet of plastic with a coating of chemicals. As light shines on the chemicals, it changes them. An image, or picture of the light, is made on the film. The camera controls the light that changes the chemicals. The film is then *developed,* or made into a *negative*.

The image in a negative is reversed from the image in a picture. The dark shades in a black-and-white negative are the light shades in a picture. The light shades in a negative are the dark shades in a picture. A color negative has three layers of chemicals. One layer is affected by red light, another by green light, and another by blue light.

Negatives are used to make *prints*. The print is the picture itself. Black-and-white film makes black-and-white prints. Color film makes color prints.

Shining light through the negative onto special paper makes the print. The dark spots on the negative block the light. Only a little light shines on the paper. With less light, the paper makes a lighter image. The lighter spots on the negative let the light through. A lot of light shines on the paper. With more light, the paper makes a darker image. This process reverses the light and dark areas of the image. The picture is perfect!

George Eastman invented a camera in 1888. He wanted to give the camera—and film—a name that began and ended with the letter "K." It was his favorite letter and the first letter of his mother's name. Putting together different letters, he came up with the name "Kodak." Today, Kodak is a giant maker of cameras and films.

George Eastman

Color slide

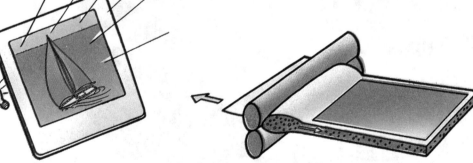
Instant film and rollers

Black-and-white print

Color print

Instant print

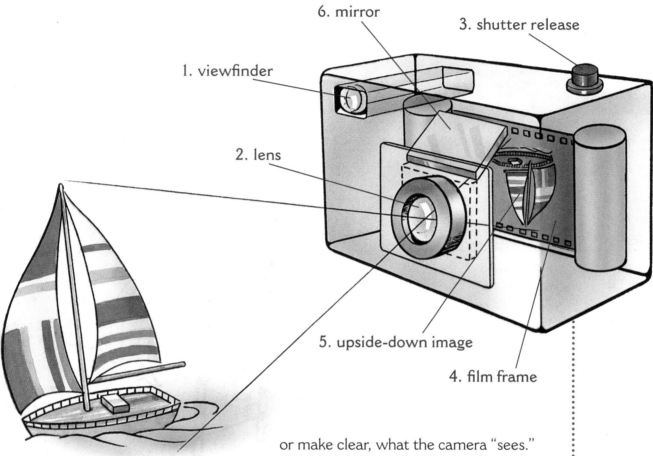

6. mirror

3. shutter release

1. viewfinder

2. lens

5. upside-down image

4. film frame

Another kind of film makes *slides*. A slide is a developed piece of film mounted in a cardboard frame. The image in a slide isn't reversed. Shining light through the slide projects an image onto the screen.

Instant cameras make a picture right away. These cameras use film that develops itself. As the film is pulled from the camera, the rollers spread chemicals that change in light over the film and paper. Light develops the picture right before your eyes.

1. Looking through the *viewfinder* lets you see the people or things you will be taking a picture of.

2. Light comes into the camera through the *lens*. A camera lens may be several small lenses. These lenses *focus*, or make clear, what the camera "sees." Light from the image must be focused onto the film so that a picture can be made. Some cameras focus themselves.

The *shutter* keeps the light from reaching the film until you are ready to take the picture. The shutter can be behind, in front of, or in the lens.

3. Pressing the *shutter release* opens and closes the shutter faster than you can see. That's enough time for the light to change the chemicals on the film.

4. The film moves through the camera *frame* by frame. A frame is the amount of film needed to take one picture.

5. The light passes through the lens and shines on the film. A camera that has one lens makes an upside-down image on the film.

6. A mirror reflects the image that is sent to the viewfinder. The image looks right-side up.

3-D Movie

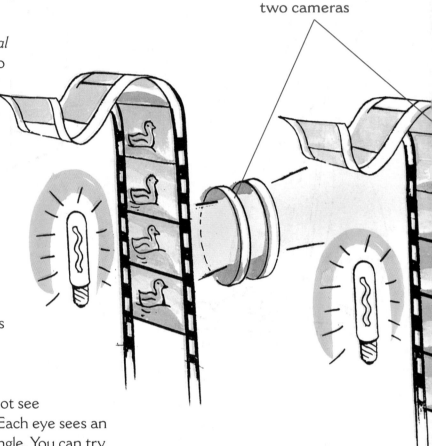

images recorded by two cameras

Movies that are *three-dimensional* have images that seem to jump off the screen. Monsters look like they are grabbing at you. Boulders seem to roll toward you. The movie comes to life!

People see in three dimensions. The dimensions are height, width, and depth. Images that have only height and width look flat. Depth makes images look three-dimensional.

We *perceive,* or see, depth because we have two eyes. Our eyes do not see exactly the same thing. Each eye sees an image from a different angle. You can try it yourself. Cover your left eye and look at something close-up. Then cover your right eye and look at the same thing. See the difference? The brain puts the two pictures together. You see one three-dimensional image.

When a 3-D movie is made, it is filmed with two cameras that are side by side. The cameras act like your two eyes. The images from the two cameras pass through polarizing filters. The images are *light waves.* Light waves vibrate in all

You can now experience 3-D in the video arcade or even at home. To play some video games, you must wear special headgear. This headgear has a little television screen for each eye. The images on the screens are different, just like the images in 3-D movies. Your brain puts them together to make the game look three-dimensional.

directions. One camera's filter only lets through the light rays that vibrate horizontally (side to side). The other camera's filter only lets through light rays that vibrate vertically (up and down). The images are combined into one film for the movie projector.

The movie projector projects the film onto the movie screen. The picture on the screen is made up of the polarized images from the two cameras.

To see the image on the screen in three dimensions, the audience has to wear 3-D glasses. The lenses of the glasses have the same polarizing filters as

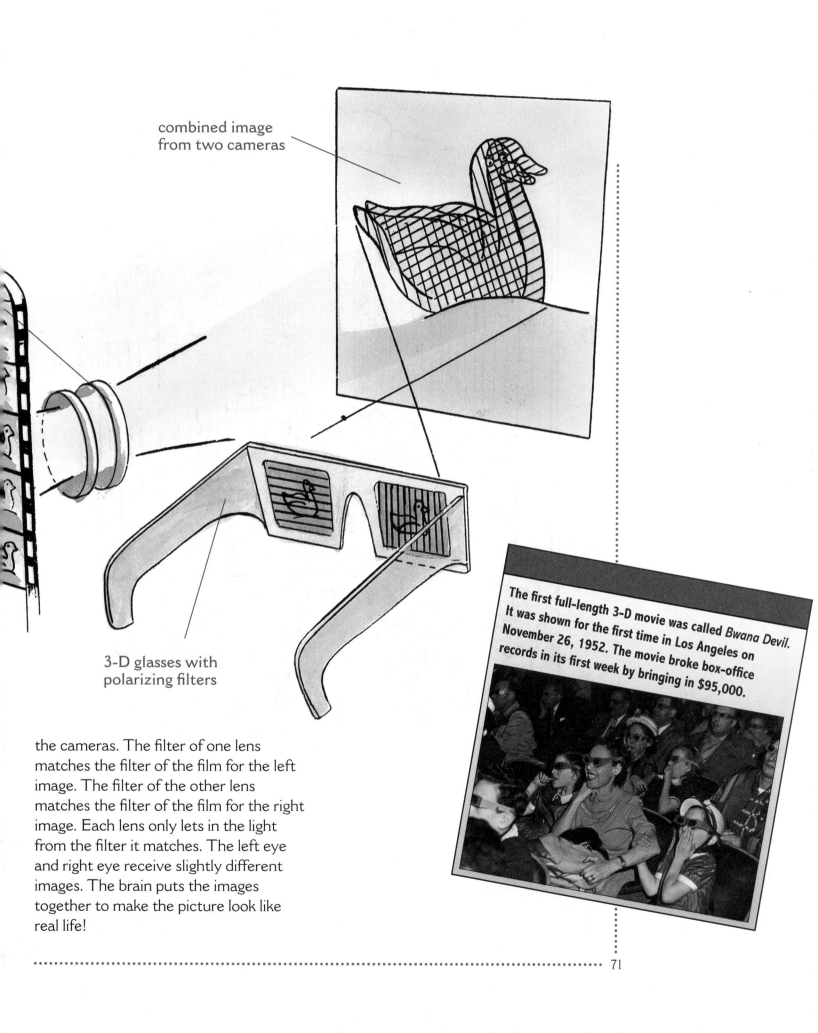

combined image
from two cameras

3-D glasses with
polarizing filters

The first full-length 3-D movie was called *Bwana Devil*. It was shown for the first time in Los Angeles on November 26, 1952. The movie broke box-office records in its first week by bringing in $95,000.

the cameras. The filter of one lens matches the filter of the film for the left image. The filter of the other lens matches the filter of the film for the right image. Each lens only lets in the light from the filter it matches. The left eye and right eye receive slightly different images. The brain puts the images together to make the picture look like real life!

Special Effects

Some movie special effects are simple to do. Running film backward *reverses* the action. For example, a swimmer jumps out of a pool backward and lands on her feet. If you stop the camera, take an actor out of the scene, and start filming again, it will look as if the actor disappeared when the film is shown.

For more complicated effects, many tricks are used together. To create a giant gorilla climbing up a building, a smaller model of the scene is used. First, a model of the building is built. It is placed in front of a background that looks real. A person wearing a gorilla suit climbs up the building. When you see the scene on a movie screen, you won't notice that the building and gorilla are really small.

See that giant lizard walking down the streets of the city? The first step in creating this special effect is to pick a background. People running away—from nothing—are filmed against the city background.

The lizard—either a real lizard or a model—is filmed in front of a special blue background. Then the two films are combined. The blue background disappears and it looks as though the lizard is walking down the city street. The lizard can be made to look enormous by showing the background buildings at a much smaller size.

Cut-out *mattes* in the shape of buildings or cars can be placed in front of the lizard. These mattes leave blank spaces on the film. Projected pictures of the buildings or cars are added later to fill

the blank spaces. The same effect can be created with a computer, by erasing part of an image and adding another image in the blank space. It looks as if the lizard is coming out from behind real buildings and cars. The final film image looks real!

Nowadays, computers are so advanced that sometimes what you see on the screen never existed. Instead of filming models or animals, the moviemakers can create images on computer and put these images onto film.

Today we have all sorts of computers and gadgets to create special effects for movies. But not long ago, moviemakers did not have the same technology. For example, take the 1951 movie *Royal Wedding*. In it, the actor and dancer Fred Astaire dances up the walls and across the ceiling. To create this special effect, a rotating room was built. All the furniture was anchored to the walls and floor. So were the cameras and camera operators! As the room turned, only the dancer stayed upright.

Cartoons

You may not realize that your eyes "remember" things. It's true! For a split second, they hold onto the last image they saw. It is eye/brain memory that makes movies—and cartoons—work.

If a picture quickly takes the place of another picture, the brain thinks it is seeing just one picture. If this happens over and over and there are slight changes in each picture, the brain thinks it is seeing a moving picture. If the pictures (called *frames)* are shown as fast as 24 frames per second, the image moves smoothly. If the pictures are shown slower than 24 frames per second, the image does not move smoothly.

A cartoon is frame after frame of drawings. An artist creates the drawings by hand using pencils, inks, and paints. Some of today's computers can create the drawings as well. No matter how the frames are created, the cartoon is still a group of changing frames.

Walt Disney

For the first Mickey Mouse cartoon, Mickey's voice was that of Walt Disney himself. Disney continued to be the voice of Mickey Mouse for the next 20 years. Believe it or not, Mickey Mouse started his career as a rabbit, Oswald the Lucky Rabbit. Oswald was a black rabbit with a white face. Except for the wrong kind of tail and ears, he looked a lot like a mouse. Because of legal problems over who had the rights to Oswald, Walt Disney decided to change the name and the type of animal. In his studio in Kansas City, Disney had a tame mouse named Mortimer. Soon, Disney was drawing Mortimer Mouse cartoons. Before his first animated cartoon was released, the name was changed to Mickey Mouse.

Drawing the frames takes a lot of time. Remember, the artist would have to draw 24 pictures for every second of film. A 90-minute film would have 129,600 drawings! It would take an artist drawing one frame every ten minutes—and that is fast—more than 11 years to draw the cartoon.

One way to cut down on the time it takes to create a cartoon is to paint on cels. Cels are clear plastic sheets. Only the changes between one frame of the cartoon and the next are painted on the cels. One (or a few) backgrounds are painted because the background changes less often. A cel is then placed over the background. The same thing is done with the next cel—which is a little different—and the next cel after that, and so on. A movie camera makes a photograph of each cel against the background. The photographs then become the frames that make up the moving cartoon. You have probably noticed that the characters on your favorite cartoon shows might show up in front of the same backgrounds over and over!

Another trick to save time is to keep each drawing simple. Cartoon characters are usually drawn with simple outlines and not much detail.

With the invention of computers came the fastest and easiest way to make cartoons. A computer can store information about how a character walks, runs, or flies. The computer then can draw the character. The computer draws the character—in single frames—walking, running, or flying.

A script is written before a cartoon can be drawn. The script describes every scene and gives the words to the story. Actors read aloud from the script and are the voices of the characters. Often, one actor is the voice for many characters. As the people read the script, the sound is recorded. The cartoonist can then draw the faces of the characters to match the words being said. The mouth of the character moves in the same ways that the reader's mouth moves.

Movie Makeup

Many make-believe movie creatures are created with *latex*. Latex is a creamy liquid that changes to a rubbery "skin." Liquid latex can be poured into a mold of any shape. It can be molded into the shape of a wrinkled forehead, a big nose, or the head of a space alien. Left to set, the liquid latex becomes solid.

When the latex is peeled out of the mold, it is painted and decorated. It is then fitted to the actor.

1. Making an actor into a space alien is easy. A mask is made for the actor to wear. A model of the actor's head is made first. The model—not the real head of the actor—is used to make the mask. Next, the head of a space alien is carved in clay over the model of the actor's head.

2. The model of the space alien's head is placed inside a shell. Plaster is poured into the shell. The plaster flows around the mold, sits, and gets hard. A thin wall sits between the front and back of the shell. The wall lets the two hardened blocks of plaster come apart so that the alien's head can be taken out.

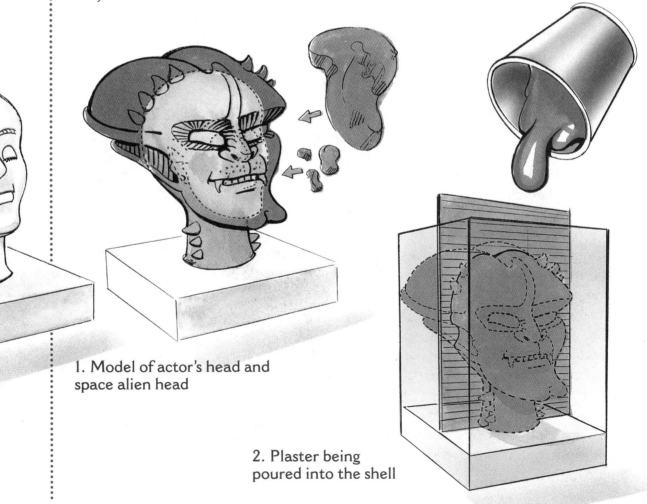

1. Model of actor's head and space alien head

2. Plaster being poured into the shell

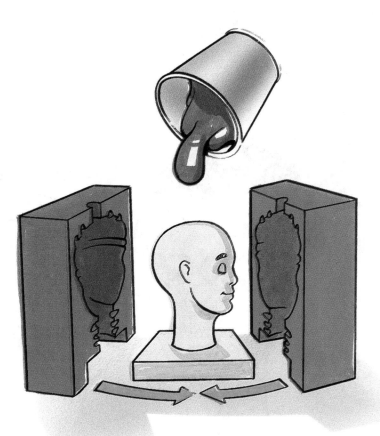

3. Pouring latex into the final mold

3. There are now two molds *imprinted* with the space alien's head. That means the molds have the marks of the space alien's head. One mold is of the alien's face. The other mold is of the back of the alien's head. The molds are then placed around the model of the actor's head.

Liquid latex is poured into the mold. It fills the space between the model head and the imprint of the alien's head. The two molds are tightly put together so that no latex leaks out.

4. When the latex has dried and hardened, the two molds are pulled apart. A mask has been made. It is a rubbery latex mold of the model of the alien's head. The mask fits like a "skin" on the actor's head. Holes will be cut into the face part of the mask so the actor will be able to see and breathe. The mask will then be painted.

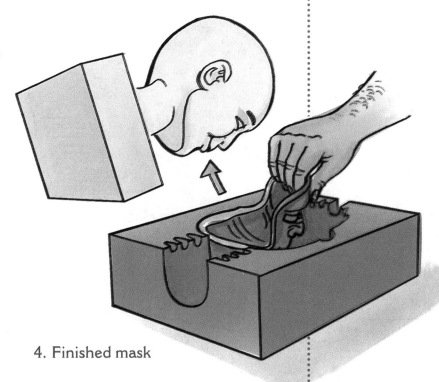

4. Finished mask

Movie Makeup

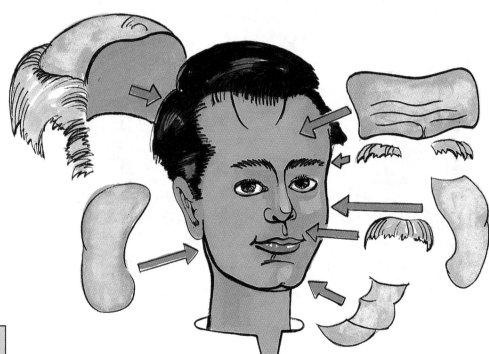

To make a young person look old, patches of latex are molded to look like wrinkled skin. The latex patches are fixed to the actor's face with a special glue. Makeup is put on over the patches and the actor's real skin to blend them together.

Topped with a wig or a latex bald head, this actor may have an idea of how he will look when he gets older!

In 1967, an out-of-work actor put on a disguise. He used movie makeup to make his face and hands look just like those of an old woman. After putting on a dress and a gray wig, he put a gun in his purse, then made his way to the local bank and held it up. A teller punched the silent alarm. On the way out, the "old lady" was surrounded by police officers and taken away. He was at the station house for more than three hours before the police realized that the bad bank robber they had arrested was really a pretty good actor.

Videocassette Recorder

The tapes that go into a videocassette recorder (VCR) are plastic strips coated with magnetic metal particles. A VCR records the picture from the TV on *tracks* (paths). The picture tracks run diagonally across the tape. The VCR records the sound from the TV on a straight track. The *electromagnets* that record and play the tape are called *heads*. (An electromagnet is a core, or center, of metal with wire wrapped around it. When electricity flows through the wire, the core turns into a magnet.)

The VCR is connected by *cables* (wires similar to ropes) to the antenna and to the TV set. Pushing the videocassette into the VCR flips a plastic flap up. The machine's arms pull a loop of the tape out of the cassette and wrap it around the recording/playback head. When you record a program, the *tuner* picks up the TV signals to be recorded from the antenna. The recording/playback head arranges the particles of metal into a magnetic pattern that matches the signals for the picture. Another head records the sound signals.

When you play the tape, the magnetic patterns produce the picture signals through the

recording/playback head. The tuner then changes the VCR signals into TV signals. The signals are sent to the TV set.

antenna

videocassette

cables

Video recording was invented in 1928 by John L. Baird, one of the pioneers of television. The first recordings were made on 78 rpm discs. The same kind of discs were used on the record players of the day.

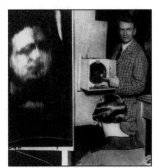

John L. Baird demonstrates his early TV. The TVs we watch today use technology developed by a different inventor.

Television

In September 1953, many television screens in England suddenly showed the call letters of TV station KLEE. KLEE was in Houston, Texas, more than 5,000 miles from England. At the time, TV signals could travel only about 150 miles. It was impossible to send a program from anywhere in the United States to England. It was a strange event that got even stranger. When people in England wrote to station KLEE to tell what they had seen, they got some startling news. Station KLEE had gone off the air three years before! Since that time, no KLEE call letters had ever been shown. What's the explanation? Some scientists believe TV signals do not always simply leave Earth and go out into space. Instead, some of them might go around and around the planet, orbiting it for years.

Television systems have three basic parts. They are a television camera, a *transmitter,* and a *receiver* (your TV set). These three parts work together to bring a scene from a television studio into your home.

A television camera takes 30 pictures per second. The pictures are flashed so fast they look as if they make up one moving image. A microphone picks up the sound that goes with the pictures.

A color television camera separates the picture into three images. One image is of all the red color in a scene. Another image is of all the blue color in a scene. And the third is of all the green color in a scene. Each image goes to a *tube.* The tubes change the pictures into electrical signals. These TV signals travel through wires to a transmitter. Sometimes the signals travel to a videotape recorder. Then the TV show can be *transmitted,* later. "Transmit" means "to send."

The TV station uses a transmitter to send the signals to your home. The transmitter sends the signals through the air in all directions.

Your TV's antenna picks up the signals from the air. It sends the signals to the tuner built into the TV set. The tuner receives the signals. The tuner picks out only the signals for the channel you want to watch. It changes the TV signals into *video,* or picture, signals. It also separates the *audio,* or sound, signals from the picture.

The tuner then sends the audio signal to the *amplifier* and the *speaker* that are

built into the set. The amplifier makes the signal stronger. The speaker turns the signal into sound you can hear and understand.

From the tuner, the video signal goes to a *decoder.* The decoder picks out the separate red, blue, and green signals that make up the image. It sends these signals to three *electron* guns. (An electron is part of an atom. An atom is a particle

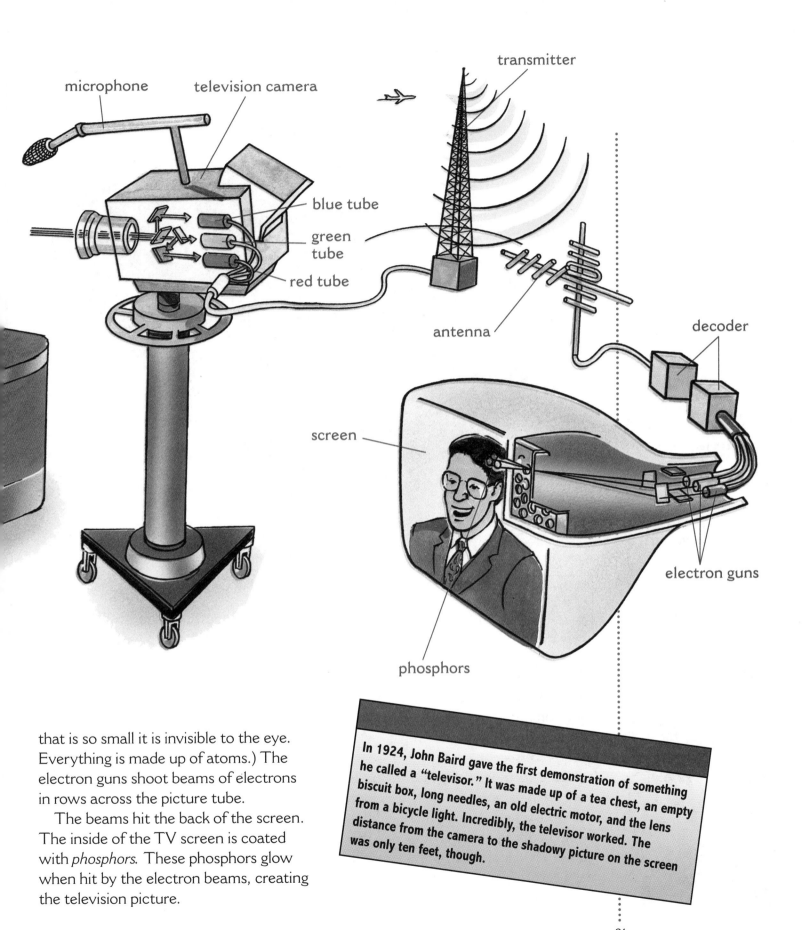

microphone

television camera

transmitter

blue tube

green tube

red tube

antenna

decoder

screen

electron guns

phosphors

that is so small it is invisible to the eye. Everything is made up of atoms.) The electron guns shoot beams of electrons in rows across the picture tube.

The beams hit the back of the screen. The inside of the TV screen is coated with *phosphors.* These phosphors glow when hit by the electron beams, creating the television picture.

In 1924, John Baird gave the first demonstration of something he called a "televisor." It was made up of a tea chest, an empty biscuit box, long needles, an old electric motor, and the lens from a bicycle light. Incredibly, the televisor worked. The distance from the camera to the shadowy picture on the screen was only ten feet, though.

Video Games

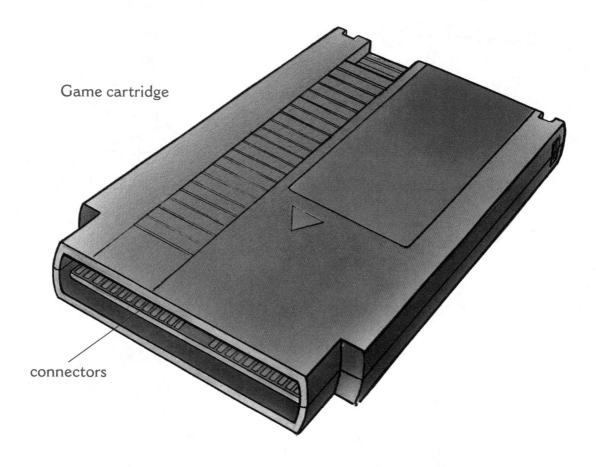

Game cartridge

connectors

People can really get involved in video games! In Phoenix, Arizona, a boy and his dad were home alone playing a game of Space Invaders. It was a close, tense match. The two were so wrapped up in it that they didn't realize their house was on fire until the fire engines screamed to a halt outside in the street.

Most video game systems are made of a *base unit, game cartridges,* and *controls* (like a joystick). The base unit holds a small computer. The computer uses *microchips* to work. One computer chip is the brain of the system. The brain chip is the *microprocessor.*

Game cartridges plug into the base unit. Each game cartridge has its own computer chips. These chips hold the computer programs that make up the game. The metal strips at the end of each cartridge are *connectors.* They connect the chips inside the cartridge to

the microprocessor inside the base unit. The game cartridge also has information about sound and pictures.

The video game controls hold many switches. These switches are often buttons and levers. One control makes the characters move around the screen. It is really four switches in one. Each time you push the control to the left, you push down on the left switch. The left switch sends a pulse into the system. The pulse is a signal. The pulse tells the microprocessor to move the character to the left. The same thing happens when you press the up, down, and right buttons. When you press buttons to fire a missile or start over, they send pulses to the microprocessor, too.

The microprocessor changes the commands you give with the joystick into the sounds you hear and pictures you see on the TV screen. Once the microprocessor understands the commands, it sends commands to two other chips in the base unit. One chip is the pictures chip. The pictures chip makes the characters look like they are moving. The other chip is the sound chip. The sound chip makes music and sound effects.

Many video games can also be played on computers. Some games are educational, and some are just for fun. They are all *interactive.* They give you choices to make and things to do.

In interactive games, you might explore lands, castles, or caves. As you play, you have to tell the computer what you want it to do. Do you want your character to look around, dig, or jump over a pit? If you don't do the right thing, you might miss finding the treasure or your character might fall off a cliff.

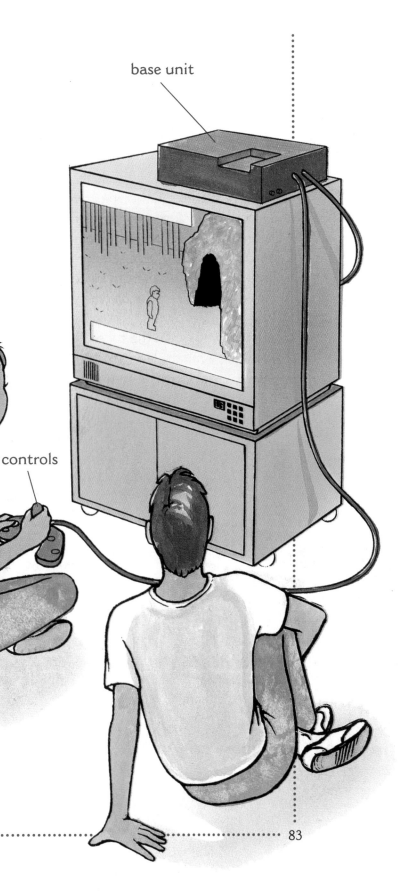

base unit

controls

Telescope

A special kind of telescope, called a reflecting telescope, uses mirrors and lenses to magnify an image. The Hubble Space Telescope is a reflecting telescope that orbits Earth. Astronomers use it to look at planets, stars, and galaxies. It sends image information to Earth using radio waves.

A simple kind of telescope is made of two tubes and three lenses. One of the tubes fits inside the other. A large glass lens is at one end of the tubes. It is the *objective*. The objective points at the *object*. Light rays travel from an object to the objective. As these light rays pass through the objective, they form a tiny, close-up image of the distant object. This occurs because light rays bend when they pass from one material to another, such as from air to glass. The image formed by the objective is upside-down.

Halfway down the tube is a middle lens. The middle lens bends the light waves again, this time turning the image right-side up. The image reaches the next lens right-side up.

The *eyepiece* is the lens near the eye. It bends the light again, making the tiny image look bigger. An eyepiece can be made up of one lens or many lenses. The lenses of a telescope working together can have great magnifying power.

One of the tubes slides in and out of the other so the telescope can be *focused*. Focusing means making something look clear. Sliding the tube changes the distance between the objective and the eyepiece. When this distance is just right, the image becomes focused. The image of the object seen through the telescope is clear.

In 1924, astronomer William Pickering observed a number of dark spots on the moon through a telescope. He had a weird theory to account for them. He said the dark spots were enormous swarms of insects moving around on the moon's surface. Now, of course, we know that the spots are shadows cast by crater rims.

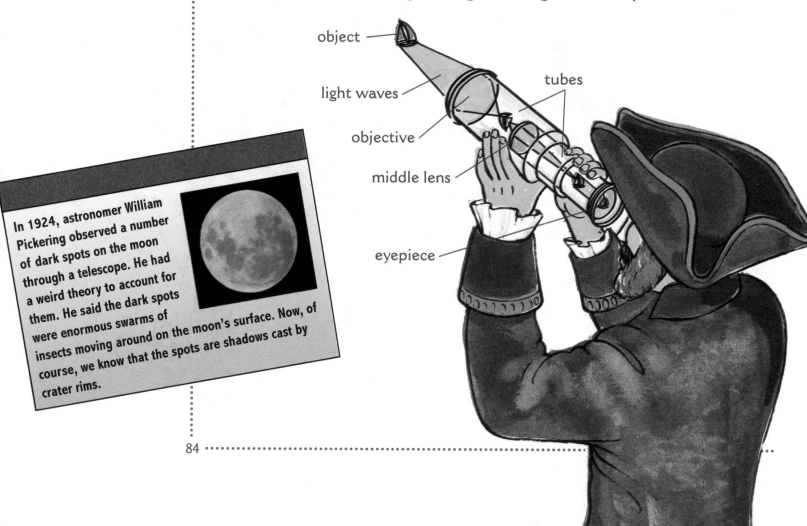

object

light waves

objective

middle lens

tubes

eyepiece

X-ray Machine

X rays are a kind of energy. They travel in waves, just like light, but we cannot see X rays. They can travel through some things, but not through others.

Pictures can be taken with an X-ray machine. The machine uses X rays, instead of the light we can see, to take pictures.

X rays are produced in a tube. The tube has electricity flowing through it. *Particles,* or tiny pieces, from the flowing electricity make a beam. The beam is shot at a piece of metal inside the tube. When the particles hit the metal, they give off energy, making X rays. The X rays are powerful. The X rays leave the machine through a window.

The X rays travel to the patient. X rays can pass through soft human tissues—like skin—but they cannot pass through bone. The bone absorbs the rays like a sponge absorbs water.

When a leg is put between the X-ray machine and a piece of X-ray film, the rays pass through the soft parts of the leg and go on to the film. The bones in the leg absorb the X rays. The film is darker everywhere the rays hit it. The film makes a picture of the bone's shadow and not the bone itself.

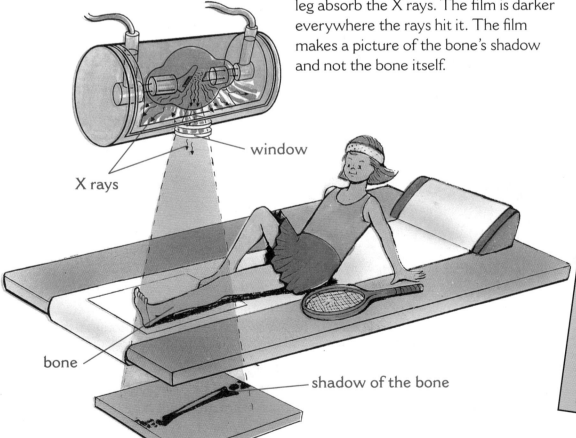

window

X rays

bone

shadow of the bone

film

News of the invention of the X ray in 1896 by Wilhelm Roentgen made many people nervous. A rumor spread that the new discovery would enable people to see through clothing. A New Jersey assemblyman was certain the rumor was true. To protect "the public from being spied on through their garments," he introduced a bill outlawing the use of X rays in opera glasses. The bill was voted down by others with a clearer picture of what the new device was all about.

Microscope

sually, if you're trying to look at something very small, you hold it up close to your eyes. But our eyes cannot *focus* on, or clearly see, things that are too close. Try it yourself: Hold a coin an inch from your right eye while the left one is closed. The coin is blurry. Slowly move the coin away from your eye. It becomes clear.

The part of the eye on which the image is seen is the *retina*. The retina is like a movie screen on the back wall of the eyeball. Holding something very close to your

When an object is within the focal length of the lens, the object looks bigger.

eye makes the image on the retina big. But the eye cannot focus on the image.

A magnifying glass can help you see very small objects. It bends the light waves from an object's image. The image is made bigger before it reaches the retina of the eye. The eye focuses on this bigger image.

The lens of a magnifying glass is *converging*. Converging means that the

glass bends light rays so they come together at a point. That point is the *focal point*. When an object is between the focal point and the lens, its image looks bigger in the lens. It also appears to be farther away than it would be without the magnifying glass. The distance between the magnifying glass and the focal point is the *focal length*.

A microscope can help you see objects that are even smaller, ones you could not see at all with just your eyes. A compound microscope uses more than one lens to magnify the image of an object that is too small to see.

1. There first must be enough light to see the object.

2. Light—daylight or electric—is directed up into the microscope by a mirror. The mirror can be moved to change the amount of light that enters the microscope.

3. Because the object you are looking at must let the light pass through it, it is sliced very thin. This slice is a sample of the object. This kind of sample is called a *specimen*. The specimen is placed on a clear glass *slide*.

4. The *platform* has clips to hold the slide in place.

5. The light shines through the specimen and into the *objective lens*. The objective lens is the first lens. It *enlarges* the image, or makes it bigger. The image can be many times bigger than the size of the object.

6. Microscopes often have several objective lenses. By turning the *turret*,

you can choose objectives that will make the image up to 100 times the size of the object.

7. After the image is made bigger by the objective, it goes to the *ocular lens*. The ocular lens is the eyepiece. You look at the slide through the ocular lens. It can enlarge the image by ten times. So if you're using an objective lens that magnifies the image 20 times, the image you see through the eyepiece is 200 times bigger than the real specimen ($20 \times 10 = 200$)!

8. The focusing knob changes the distance between the objective lens and the ocular lens. When you find the correct distance, you will see the image clearly.

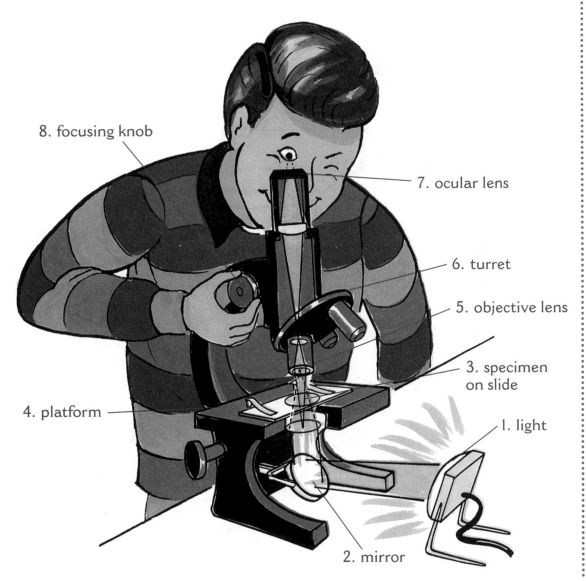

8. focusing knob

7. ocular lens

6. turret

5. objective lens

3. specimen on slide

4. platform

1. light

2. mirror

In 1590, Antonie van Leeuwenhoek, a Dutch cloth-maker and amateur scientist, built a microscope that could magnify objects to 270 times their normal size. In one of his first experiments, he scraped plaque from his own teeth. When he put the plaque under the lens, he was amazed to see what he described as "tiny animals." He wrote: "There are more animals in my mouth than there are people in all of Holland!" The "animals," of course, were bacteria.

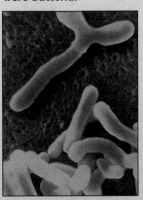

These bacteria, seen here through a microscope, usually live inside the human digestive system.

Hologram

The image on a hologram seems to float in space, solid and real. You may have seen a hologram on a credit card. Like a photograph, a hologram records picture information, but a hologram makes an image look *three-dimensional*, as if it has a solid shape.

To make a hologram, you shine a beam of light from a laser onto a *beam splitter*. The beam splitter splits the laser light so that you now have two laser beams. One of the beams is reflected off a mirror, through a lens that spreads the beam, and onto the object you're making

Making a hologram

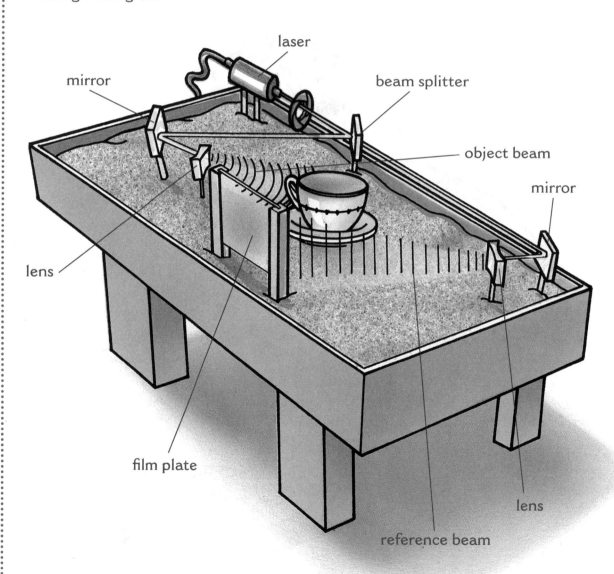

laser

mirror

beam splitter

object beam

mirror

lens

film plate

lens

reference beam

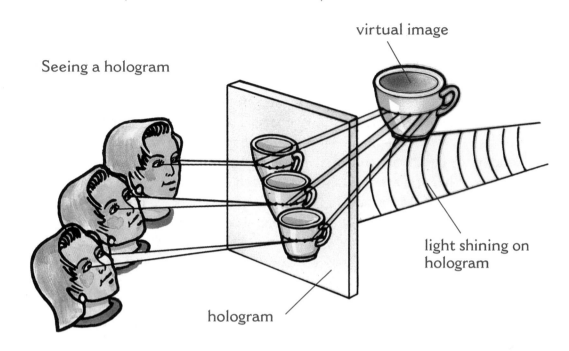

Seeing a hologram

virtual image

light shining on hologram

hologram

a picture of, such as a teacup. This beam of light is called the *object beam*. The laser light bounces off the teacup onto a *film plate*. The film plate holds a piece of film that will become the hologram.

The second laser beam that was created by the beam splitter also bounces off a mirror and goes through a lens that spreads the beam so that it is large enough to cover the entire film. This beam is called the *reference beam*.

The object beam and the reference beam make a pattern on the film. The pattern results from the light waves in the beams crossing each other. Once the film is developed, you have a hologram.

When you look at a hologram, you see a *virtual image* of the teacup—an image that appears to exist in a place where the teacup does not exist. You see light scattered by the pattern in the film. Each of your eyes sees a different set of

scattered light rays, so each eye sees a slightly different view of the teacup. Your brain combines the two images to give you a three-dimensional view. As you move your head, each eye gets changing views of the teacup, so it appears that you can look at the teacup from different angles.

The human brain sometimes creates its own holograms. They are called eidetic images. What this means is that it is possible for the human mind to actually see things that aren't there. What is seen is really a memory. For example, let's say you once had a dog, and it died. Sometime later you may suddenly see the dog "eidetically." An eidetic image looks very real to the person seeing it. Some people see things in this way more than others. Children are more likely to have eidetic images than grown-ups.

Kaleidoscope

Although the patterns seem endless and the designs look complex, the kaleidoscope is a simple invention.

At one end of the cardboard tube is a peephole. At the other end are two sheets of glass or plastic. The inside sheet is clear. The outside sheet is made of *ground glass* (glass with a foggy-looking surface) or plastic. Bits of colored glass, beads, or metal chips are sandwiched between the sheets of glass.

A pair of long, flat mirrors runs along the tube. The mirrors face each other. They make a V shape with an angle of 60 degrees. As light shines through the plates of glass, the mirrors reflect the image. The image is of the colored bits. The reflections are *repeated*—they are shown again and again. Because of repeated reflections, the mirrors show five images. The sixth image you see is of the real colored glass bits, beads, or metal chips. Peeping through the hole, you see the same colored design six times.

When you turn the tube, the colored pieces move, forming a brand-new pattern.

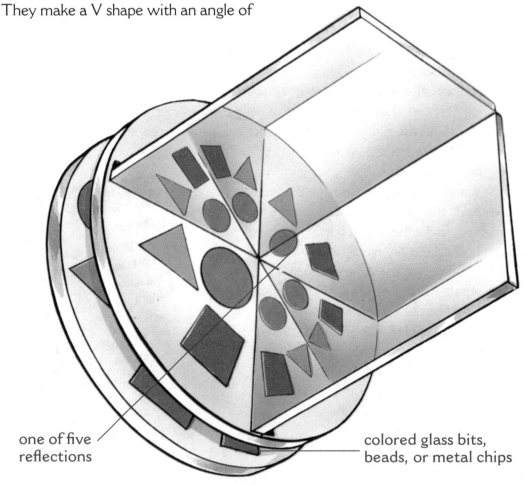

one of five
reflections

colored glass bits,
beads, or metal chips

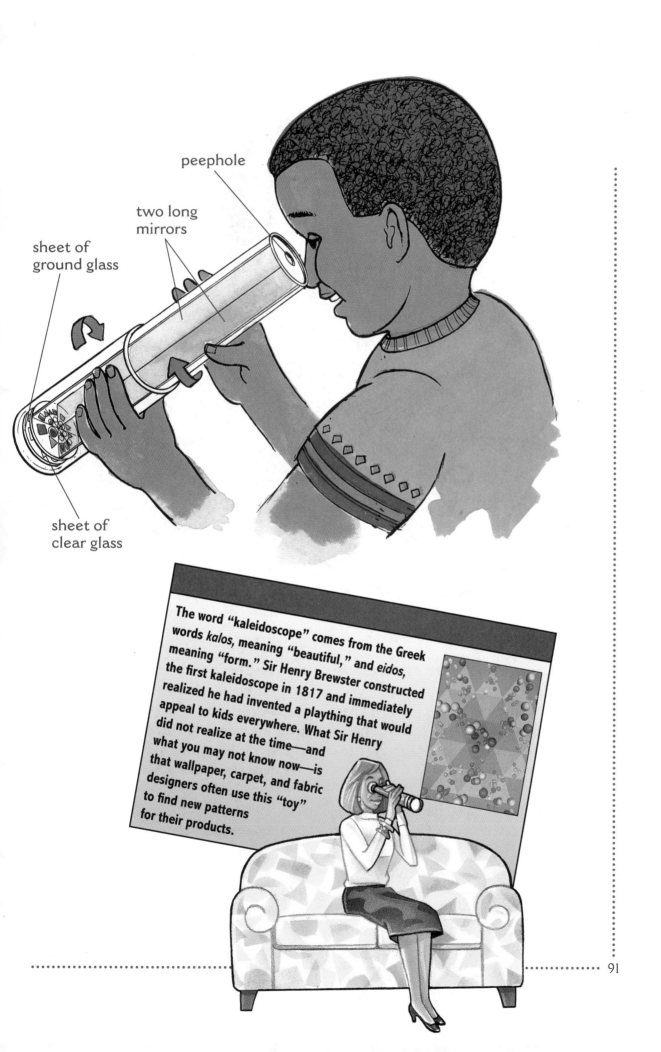

peephole

two long
mirrors

sheet of
ground glass

sheet of
clear glass

The word "kaleidoscope" comes from the Greek words *kalos*, meaning "beautiful," and *eidos*, meaning "form." Sir Henry Brewster constructed the first kaleidoscope in 1817 and immediately realized he had invented a plaything that would appeal to kids everywhere. What Sir Henry did not realize at the time—and what you may not know now—is that wallpaper, carpet, and fabric designers often use this "toy" to find new patterns for their products.

Eyeglasses

The first eyeglasses were held in front of the eyes by a handle. Other eyeglasses were tied to the head by a ribbon. Still other glasses clipped onto the nose like a clothespin.

For a person to see an image well, the image must be *focused,* or shown clearly, inside the eye. The image should focus on the eye's *retina*. The retina is like a movie screen on the back wall of the eyeball. Light from an object enters the eye through the *cornea,* the eye's clear outer layer. Behind the cornea is the clear eye *lens* that focuses light on the retina. The *iris* gives eyes their color. The *pupil* is the black center opening of the iris.

Some people are *farsighted.* What they see far away looks clear. What they

see close up looks blurry. Other people are *nearsighted.* What they see close up looks clear. What they see far away looks blurry. Eyeglass lenses of different shapes clear up the blurry images.

Convex lenses help farsighted people see up close. Convex lenses curve out. *Concave* lenses help nearsighted people see far away. Concave lenses curve in.

Here's how these lenses help correct poor vision. The shape of a farsighted eye is shorter than the shape of a normal eye. When it looks at a close-up object, it forms an image. This image focuses

92

behind, not on, the retina. The brain sees a fuzzy picture. A faraway object focuses on the retina. The brain sees a clear picture. A lens that makes a close-up image seem farther away will help the eye see better.

A convex lens bends light rays in. The rays seem to come from farther away. The light can then be focused on the retina as in a normal eye. The farsighted eye then clearly sees things near and far.

The shape of a nearsighted eye is longer than the shape of a normal eye. When it looks at a faraway object, it forms an image. This image focuses in front of, not on, the retina. Again, the brain sees a fuzzy picture. A close-up image focuses on the retina. The brain sees a clear picture. A lens that makes a faraway image seem closer will help the eye see better.

A concave lens bends light rays out. The rays seem to come from close up. The light can then be focused on the retina as in a normal eye. The nearsighted eye then clearly sees things far and near.

Uncorrected farsightedness   Corrected farsightedness

retina   lens   cornea   convex lens

Uncorrected nearsightedness   Corrected nearsightedness

retina   lens   cornea   concave lens

Mirror

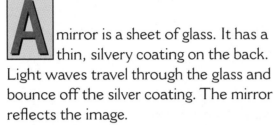

A mirror is a sheet of glass. It has a thin, silvery coating on the back. Light waves travel through the glass and bounce off the silver coating. The mirror reflects the image.

When you are looking straight into a mirror, your image is exactly the opposite of you. Light waves hit the mirror in one direction. They bounce off the mirror at the same angle and in the opposite direction. The image looks *reversed*. You have seen it yourself many times. Look in a mirror and wave your right hand. The image in the mirror will wave its left hand back at you.

A *two-way mirror* lets people on one side see through it—like a window—while people on the other side see only a mirror. Two-way mirrors have a thinner silver coating than a regular mirror has. In front of the mirror is a brightly lighted room. (The front of the mirror is the side without the coating.) Behind the mirror is a darker room. The person behind the

Two-way mirror

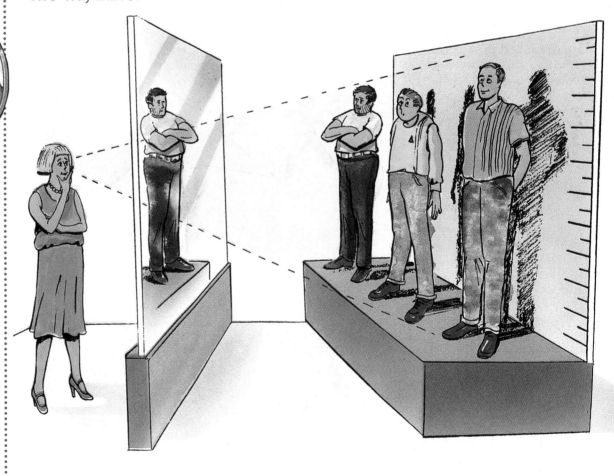

mirror can see through the back of the mirror. The people in front of the mirror see only their reflections.

A *concave mirror* curves up at the edges. The curve makes the reflected image look bigger than the object. But you see a smaller area than if the mirror was flat.

The glass of a *convex mirror* curves down at the edges. This curve makes the reflected image look smaller than the object. But you see a bigger area than if the mirror was flat.

Convex mirror

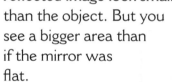

Flat mirror

Concave mirror

Long ago in China, people placed mirrors near the roofs of their houses. The Chinese people believed the mirrors would reflect away evil things.

Doorbells, Horns, and Sirens

A doorbell isn't really a bell. It is a *chime*. A chime makes a sound that is like a bell's sound. The sound is made by a metal *striker* hitting one or more *chime plates*.

Pressing the button of the doorbell closes a switch. Closing a switch lets electricity flow to an *electromagnet*. An electromagnet is a core, or center, of metal with wire wrapped around it. When electricity flows through the wire, the metal core turns into a magnet. The electromagnet pulls the striker to one of the chime plates. It makes a musical sound. When the doorbell button is released, the electricity is switched off. The electromagnet stops pulling the striker. A spring pushes the striker back the other way. The striker hits the other

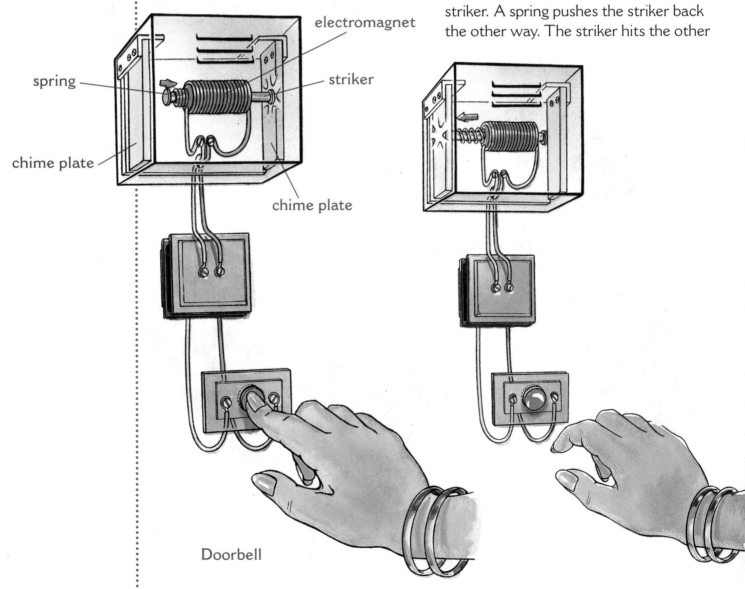

electromagnet

spring

striker

chime plate

chime plate

Doorbell

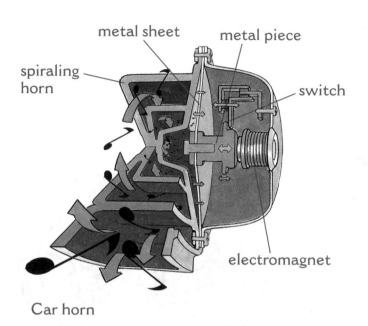

metal sheet

metal piece

spiraling horn

switch

electromagnet

Car horn

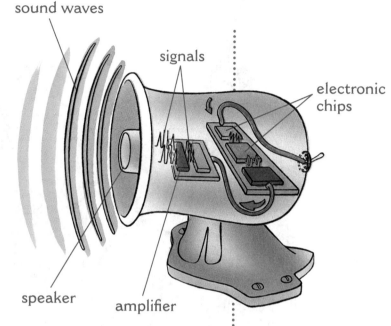

sound waves

signals

electronic chips

speaker

amplifier

Siren

chime plate. Another musical sound is made. The chimes may be tuned differently. One chime may make a high sound. The other may make a low sound.

A car horn also uses an electromagnet. Usually the horn button is in the middle of the steering wheel. Pressing the button closes a switch. Closing the switch lets the electricity flow to the electromagnet. The electromagnet pulls a metal piece. The metal piece is fixed to a thin metal sheet. As the electromagnet pulls the metal piece, it shuts off the electricity. The metal piece springs back, turning the electricity on. This step is repeated many, many times a second. Repeating this step makes the metal sheet *vibrate*. (To vibrate is to move back and forth.) The metal sheet makes a high sound as it vibrates. The sound travels through the horn. The horn is shaped like a spiral. The sound is made louder and louder as it travels toward the opening.

Sirens can make many sounds. They can make noises like cries and squeals. They can play the sound from a radio. And they can sound like normal sirens.

Inside the siren, electronic chips make signals. The signals go to an *amplifier*. The amplifier makes the signals louder. A speaker changes the signals into sounds and sends them out into the air for you to hear.

The greatest noisemaker is nature itself. On August 27, 1883, the island volcano of Krakatoa exploded. The sound of the explosion was the loudest in recorded history. It was heard 1,800 miles away in the Philippines, 1,900 miles away in Australia, and 2,000 miles away in India. Four hours after the explosion, the sound reached the tiny island of Rodrigues in the Indian Ocean, 3,000 miles from Krakatoa.

Krakatoa today

Stringed Instruments

Bass

Viola

Violin

Cello

A musician has to do two things to play a stringed instrument. The musician must set one or more of the strings into motion and control the amount of string that moves. Plucking the string with a finger or drawing a bow across the string makes it move. Pressing the string with a finger controls the amount of string that moves.

Each kind of stringed instrument makes a different kind of sound. Some sound like deep growls; some sound like sweet songs. An instrument's sound depends on many things. Its size and shape, the material of which it is made,

the kind of strings it has, and how it is played are just some of the things that affect the sound an instrument makes.

A violin is explained here. Other instruments that look like a violin are the viola, the violoncello (or just cello), and the bass viol (or just bass).

1. A violin is played by drawing a *bow* across its four strings. The bow can be strung with different materials. As the bow string rubs against the string of the violin, the violin string moves back and forth. It *vibrates*.

2. The four strings of the violin are stretched over a curved *bridge*.

3. The vibration of the string is made stronger by the body of the violin. The vibration of the string travels through the bridge and into the *soundboard*. The soundboard is the wooden top of the violin. A post connects the soundboard to the back of the violin. Both the soundboard and the back of the violin vibrate with the string. The violin's front and back are much bigger than the string—they make the vibration loud enough to hear.

4. The sound comes out through holes in the top of the violin. The sound of the string depends on how long it is and how tight it is. The shorter the string is, the higher the sound. The tighter the string is, the higher the sound.

5. By pressing a string against the *neck,* the violinist only allows the part of the string between the finger and the bridge to vibrate. Moving the fingers up and down the neck changes the amount of string that can vibrate.

Pressing a finger to the neck of the violin shortens the amount of string that can vibrate. The shortened string makes a high sound. Not pressing a finger to the neck of the violin keeps the amount of string that can vibrate long. The long string makes a low sound.

6. Each string is wound around a *peg* in the *pegbox*. The pegbox is at the end of the neck. Turning the pegs to tighten or loosen the strings *tunes* the strings. Tuning an instrument means adjusting the strings so that they make the right sounds. Tightening makes the sounds higher. Loosening makes the sounds lower.

In 1767, Englishman George Noel constructed the largest stringed instrument of all time. Called a "pantaleon," it was played with wooden mallets, like a xylophone. The instrument was made of 276 gut and metal strings stretched over a horizontal soundboard that was 11 feet long by five feet wide.

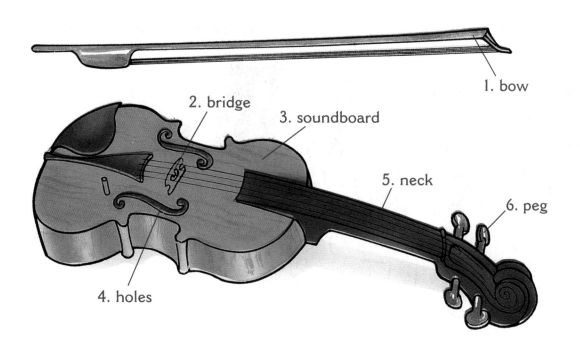

1. bow

2. bridge

3. soundboard

5. neck

6. peg

4. holes

Wind Instruments

Wind instruments use air pressure to make musical sounds. Most wind instruments are tubes through which air is blown. The air inside the tube is made to *vibrate*—to move back and forth.

Different vibrations make different sounds. A high-speed vibration makes a high note. A low-speed vibration makes a low note. These high and low speeds are *pitches* of notes. The length of the *air column* inside an instrument changes its pitch. The air column is the distance air travels before leaving the tube. The levers, holes, and slides on wind instruments change the length of the air column. Some instruments are very short. They will never sound deep and low. And some are long. They will never blow a high note.

The wind instruments shown here are the flute, the saxophone, the clarinet, and the trombone.

A trombone is a *brass* instrument. A brass instrument has a cup-shaped mouthpiece. The musician blows through the mouthpiece. The lips must be held just right to make the air inside the tube vibrate. A trombone player moves a slide in and out to change the length of the tube. With the slide out, the air travels farther before it leaves. The note is low. With the slide pulled in, the note is high.

A musician playing a brass instrument also can change the pitch by changing lip position and by blowing harder or softer. This takes a lot of practice.

Oboes and clarinets are *woodwind* instruments. Covering the holes on its side changes the length of the air column of a woodwind. On an oboe or a clarinet, pressing levers and keys covers the holes. The more holes that are covered, the farther the air must go to escape. The farther the air goes, the

Flute

Saxophone

Clarinet

Trombone

Trombone

Oboe

lower the note. When only the hole nearest the lips is open, the note is high. The lowest note is played with all the holes covered.

Some woodwinds have *reeds* fixed to their mouthpieces. A reed is a thin piece of cane or wood that vibrates when air is blown over it. Oboes and clarinets are reed instruments. The double reed of the oboe is its mouthpiece. A clarinet has one reed. The vibrating reed creates the air vibration that makes the tone in a reed instrument.

A flute has just a hole across which the musician blows air. Blowing air across this hole at the right angle starts the air vibrating inside the flute. The notes are made higher and lower by covering and opening the holes with keys and levers.

Flute

Piano and Harp

keys

pedals

The record for the longest piano-playing session was set by David Scott May in 1982. With four hours of rest a day, May played for 1,218 hours—that is more than 50 days.

A piano has 88 *keys*. Some are white and some are black. Inside the piano, the keys connect to levers, cushions, wires, and hammers. A metal frame inside the piano holds a row of wires. The wires are stretched on the frame. Under the wires is a piece of wood. The wires are the strings of the piano and the wood is the sounding board. Together, the strings and the *sounding board* give a piano its special sound.

Pressing the key drives the *hammer* against the string. The hammer falls back into place right away. A *check* keeps the hammer from bouncing back up to the string and hitting it again. A tiny spring underneath raises the key as soon as the key is let go.

When the hammer hits the string, a sound is made. The sound is different with each key that is played.

Although a piano has 88 keys on the outside, it has more than 200 strings on the inside. The deep notes are

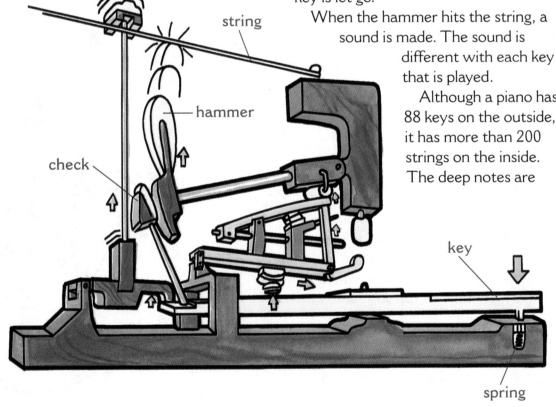

string

hammer

check

key

spring

each made by a string wrapped in wire. The middle notes are each made by two strings played at once. The highest notes are each made by three very fine strings played at once. One of the strings alone would not make a sound loud enough to be heard.

Lifting the top of a grand piano lets the sound from the sounding board bounce off the top and travel toward the audience. The pedals control *dampers*. Dampers can soften the piano's tone or make it louder and more lasting.

A harp has 47 strings. Each string plays a different note. A short string has a higher sound than a long string. Plucking the strings with a finger makes the strings *vibrate*. (To vibrate is to move back and forth.) The sound of a string comes from its vibrations.

The strings are stretched on a frame. They all end in an empty box called a *soundbox*. The soundbox makes the vibrations of the strings louder and fuller.

The tops of the strings are caught between sets of pegs. One set of pegs sits on each disk. Pressing a pedal turns the disk. As the disk turns, it shortens the length of a string, making the sound slightly higher.

pegs

disks

strings

soundbox

pedals

In ancient Egypt, only men were allowed to play the harp. For reasons we do not know, women were strictly forbidden from playing the instrument.

Electronic Keyboard

Music is a special form of sound. Sound is made up of *air vibrations.* An air vibration is the back-and-forth movement of air. Air vibrations can be changed into electrical signals by a microphone. The electrical signals are changed back into sound by a loudspeaker.

An electronic keyboard can make the electrical signals itself, without the original sound or a microphone.

All notes have different *frequencies.* Frequencies are the speeds of the air vibrations. Notes can be made up of one frequency or many different ones. This is why a trumpet sounds different from a guitar—even when they play the same note.

An electronic keyboard can sound like different instruments because it can make electrical signals that have the

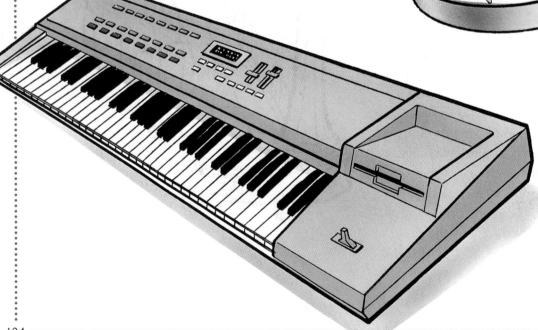

same note speed, size, and shape as many instruments. The electrical signals go from the keyboard to an *amplifier*, which makes the sounds louder, and on to the speakers. What comes out of the speaker sounds the same as what an instrument would sound like.

Keyboards can even make sounds that an instrument can't make. A keyboard can record real sounds with a microphone. The sound may be a voice, a knock at the door, or a bird's chirp. The keyboard's memory "remembers" the sound and can change it. For example, the keyboard can record a bird chirping, and play back what sounds like a bird singing "Happy Birthday!"

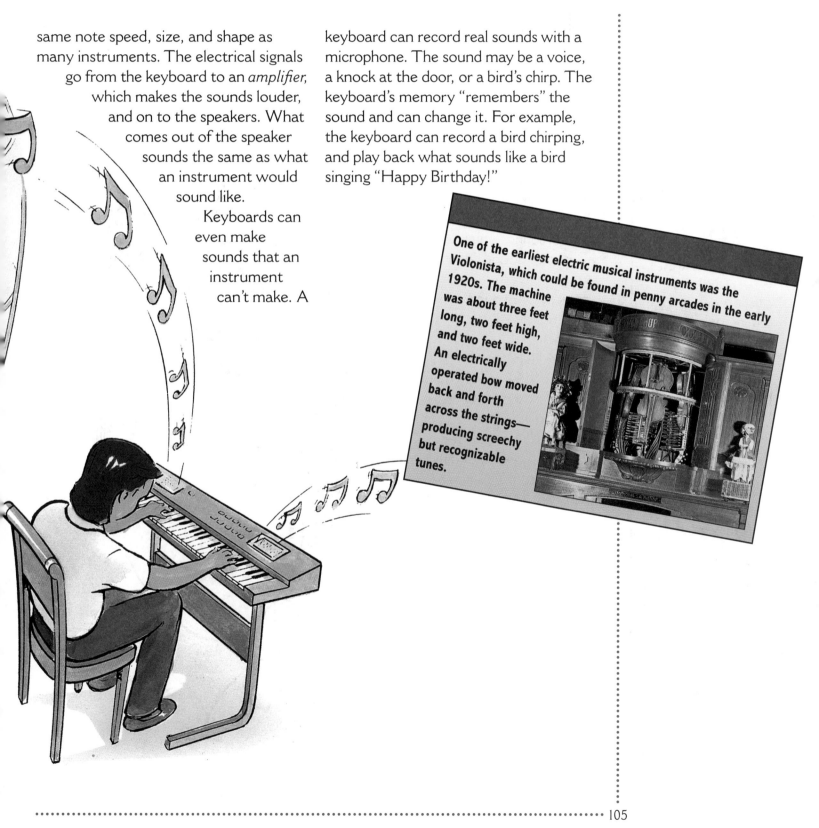

One of the earliest electric musical instruments was the Violonista, which could be found in penny arcades in the early 1920s. The machine was about three feet long, two feet high, and two feet wide. An electrically operated bow moved back and forth across the strings—producing screechy but recognizable tunes.

Stereophonic Sound

The first stereo was pretty strange. Microphones were used to record operas and other live musical performances. People who wanted to hear the recordings could rent a special gadget with two telephone receivers. Listeners held the receivers up to their ears to hear half the music through one receiver and half through the other.

The sounds you hear every day come at you from all directions. A sound does not only come to you straight from the *source*. (The source is the thing that makes the sound.) A sound can bounce off a wall or a ceiling. Sound coming out of one speaker, like that from a radio, comes from only one direction. It does not sound like the sounds you hear every day. Sound coming out of a stereo—called stereophonic sound—seems to come from many directions.

More than one microphone—usually many more—is used to record stereo sound. The microphones are placed where the best recording can be made. This can be to the sides of a band, on either side of an instrument—anywhere. Each microphone picks up a sound that is a little different from the sound another microphone picks up. The microphones make recordings called *sound tracks*. Each microphone adds to the stereo effect of the sound because each microphone picks up a different sound.

The tracks all come together to make the

recording. When you listen to the recording, it sounds as if the band were spread out behind the speakers. The sound seems to bounce all over. Some of the tracks come out of one speaker. Others will come out of the other speaker. Together, the sounds will be just as they are at a live concert.

Different things can be done when the sound is being recorded. Some instruments can be recorded on only one of the sound tracks. Other instruments can be switched between the tracks. It sounds as if the instruments were moving around the room.

Listening to sound through headphones is really listening to two separate speakers. A different sound comes out of each earpiece of the headphones. The two sounds come together. When they come together, they sound real.

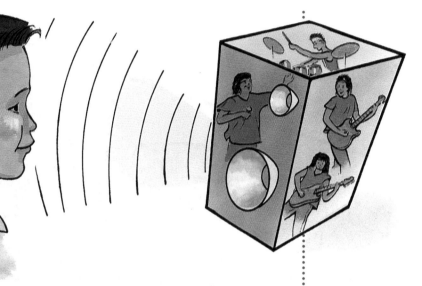

Tape Recorder and Player

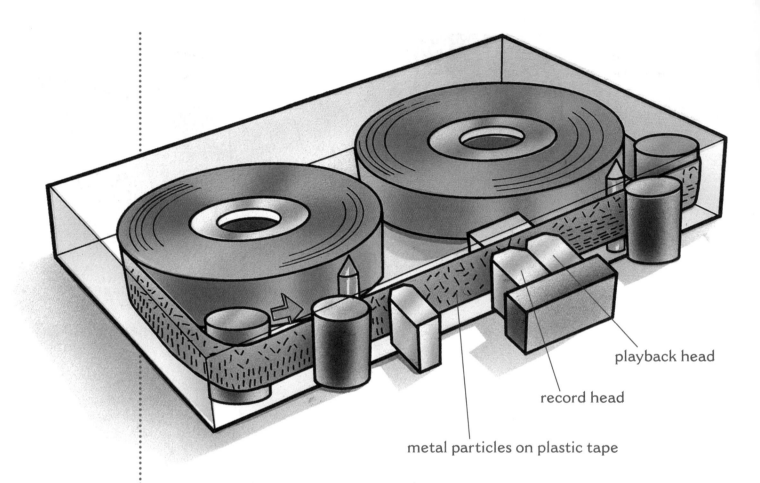

playback head

record head

metal particles on plastic tape

Sound travels through the air as waves. A tape recorder changes sound waves into electrical signals. A tape player changes the signals back into sound waves. Many machines can both record and play sound.

Sound enters the machine through the *microphone*. The microphone changes the sound into signals. The signals are electrical. Most tapes are a strip of plastic coated with a layer of magnetic metal particles. The recorder uses the electrical signals to magnetize the tape and create a magnetic signal.

During recording, the tape rubs against the *record head*. The record head is an *electromagnet*. An electromagnet is made up of a piece of metal and a coil of wire. (A coil is a loop.) The wire coil wraps around the metal. When electricity runs through the coiled wire, the metal turns into a magnet.

The magnetic signals change the pattern of the metal particles on the tape. The magnetic pattern of the metal particles matches the pattern of the electrical signals.

During playback, the machine pulls the tape across the *playback head*. The tape's magnetic signals send electricity through a coil of wire inside the head. The pattern in the flow of electricity matches the pattern of the magnetic signals. The *amplifier* makes the signals stronger. The *speaker* changes the signals into sound waves we can hear.

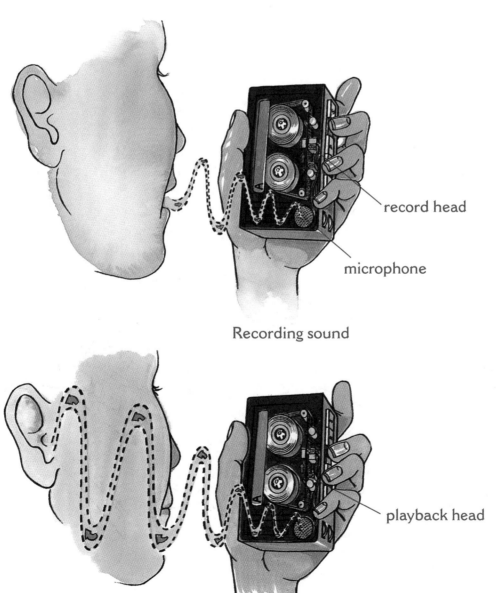

record head

microphone

Recording sound

playback head

Playing back the recording

One day in New Orleans a few years ago, a 12-year-old girl was in a store shopping for a tape recorder. While she was trying one out, a man came in and robbed the owner. The girl not only identified the man in a police lineup, she also had proof that he was the robber. She had recorded his voice during the robbery. Police used voiceprints to match the thief's voice to the tape recording.

STICK 'EM UP!

Compact Disc Player

On a compact disc, tiny pits and spaces make a pattern that spirals around the disc. The pits and spaces are on the bottom side of the CD. They serve as a code for the sounds. These pits and spaces are much too tiny to be seen with the naked eye.

During recording, the pits are pressed into the CD. The side of the CD with the pits also has a reflecting layer of aluminum and is protected by a coating of clear plastic.

During playback, a *laser* inside the compact disc player points at the bottom of the disc. (A laser is a narrow beam of high-energy light.) As the CD turns, the laser light shines on the pits and the spaces between the pits. The CD acts like a mirror. The flat spaces between pits reflect light. The pits themselves do not reflect light. The result is flickering bursts of light being reflected back into the player.

The player changes the bursts of light into electrical signals. An amplifier and speakers change the signals back into sound.

One nice thing about compact discs is that they do not wear out the way cassette tapes do. In a tape player, parts of the player rub against the tape. Bit by bit, the tape stretches and wears. The pits and spaces of a CD are read by a laser beam. They are not touched by any part of the CD player, so they do not suffer the same wear and tear as tapes.

Sometimes stories will arise about new technologies. The first CDs were 74 minutes and 33 seconds long. That was the amount of music it was practical to put on a CD. But the story goes that the music company asked the famous conductor Herbert von Karajan how long a CD should be. He is said to have answered that it should be long enough to fit Beethoven's Fifth Symphony—about 72 minutes.

laser light

Walkie-talkie

Walkie-talkies send and receive radio signals. Radio signals can go through anything except metal. With a walkie-talkie, you can sit in your room and talk to someone in another house. Walkie-talkies run on batteries and can be carried.

To send a message, you talk into the *mouthpiece*. The mouthpiece has a microphone. As you speak, you press the switch. Pressing the switch sends the message from the mouthpiece to the antenna.

As you speak into the microphone, it changes your message into electrical signals. An *amplifier* makes the electrical signals louder. A *modulator* changes these strong electrical signals into radio signals. The radio signals then go through a *signal booster*. The signal booster makes the signals stronger. Signals leave the walkie-talkie through the antenna. From there, the radio signals travel in waves through the air. The voice message has been sent.

When the radio signals hit the antenna of another walkie-talkie, they travel down into the walkie-talkie. To receive a message, you stop pressing the switch. Letting out the switch sends the message from the antenna to the

Walkie-talkie transmitting signals

radio signals

antenna

switch

mouthpiece

signal booster

modulator

amplifier

Walkie-talkie receiving signals

antenna

earpiece

switch

demodulator

earpiece. The *demodulator* changes the radio signals back into electrical signals. An amplifier makes the electrical signals stronger, then sends them to the speaker. The speaker vibrates, changing the signals back into sound. The voice message has been received.

The first wireless radio-telephones were German-made devices called *Telefunkens*. The German army used these devices during World War I. In 1933, the United States military developed the walkie-talkie. The first walkie-talkies were portable, but extremely heavy. Lugging around a 25-pound telephone was not much fun!

This U.S. soldier is using one of the earliest walkie-talkies.

Telephone

1. handset

2. earpiece and mouthpiece

Have you ever wondered how a telephone works?

1. Lifting a telephone *handset* sends a message to a phone company station. The signal travels in a split second. It says you are ready to make a call. The *dial tone*—the humming sound you hear—signals you to go ahead.

2. A handset has two jobs. In the *mouthpiece,* it changes sound waves into electricity waves. These waves will travel to the person you are calling. In the *earpiece,* the handset changes electricity waves back into sound waves, so that you can hear the person at the other end of the line.

3. Pressing push buttons on a phone sends tones (beeps) over the phone wires. The tones tell the phone company's computers where your call is going. Pressing "1" tells the computer you are making a call to someone far

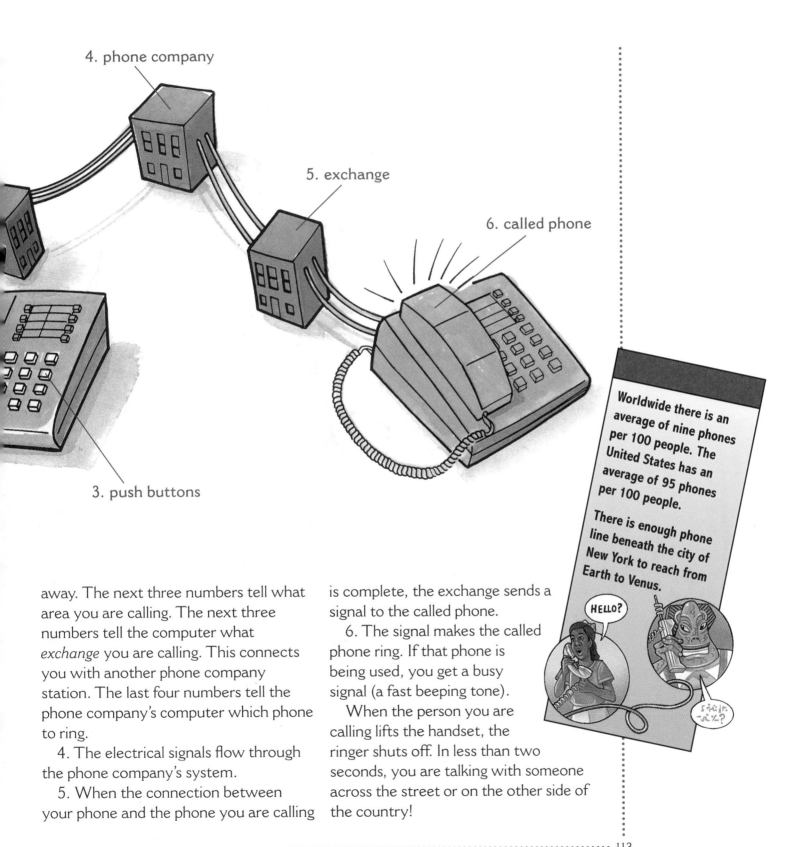

4. phone company

5. exchange

6. called phone

3. push buttons

away. The next three numbers tell what area you are calling. The next three numbers tell the computer what *exchange* you are calling. This connects you with another phone company station. The last four numbers tell the phone company's computer which phone to ring.

4. The electrical signals flow through the phone company's system.

5. When the connection between your phone and the phone you are calling is complete, the exchange sends a signal to the called phone.

6. The signal makes the called phone ring. If that phone is being used, you get a busy signal (a fast beeping tone).

When the person you are calling lifts the handset, the ringer shuts off. In less than two seconds, you are talking with someone across the street or on the other side of the country!

Worldwide there is an average of nine phones per 100 people. The United States has an average of 95 phones per 100 people.

There is enough phone line beneath the city of New York to reach from Earth to Venus.

HELLO?

113

Cellular Telephone

A regular phone has a wire that plugs into the wall, and so does the base unit of a cordless phone. But a cellular phone has no wires to connect it to anything! You can talk on a cellular phone as you ride along in a car. This kind of phone works by sending radio signals, which travel through the air.

Imagine you make a call from a regular phone to a car's cellular phone. First, the signal for the number you dial gets sent over the telephone lines to a *public telephone switching office.* You could think of this office as a place where many roads (telephone lines) come together. Your signal comes in on one "road," and it gets sent out on the right "road" to reach the person you are calling.

Since you are calling a cellular phone, the next place your signal goes is to a *mobile switching center.* From there, the signal is sent out over telephone lines or by a radio transmitter to each of the *cell sites* in the region. Each region is divided into hexagon-shaped areas called cells. The *cell site transceiver,* a tower that can send and receive radio signals, sends out a message to all cellular phones in that cell.

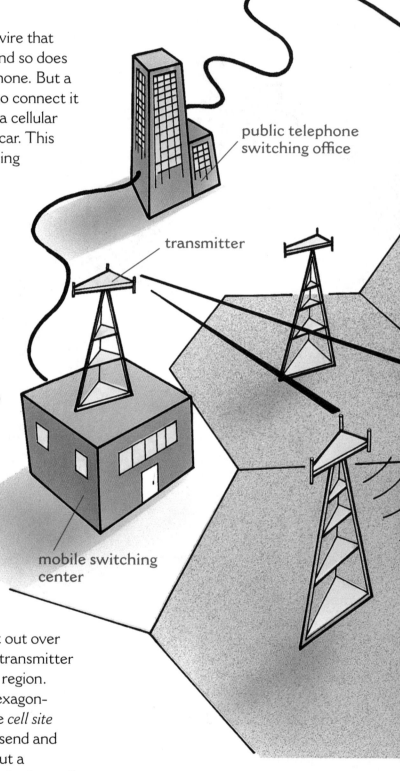

public telephone switching office

transmitter

mobile switching center

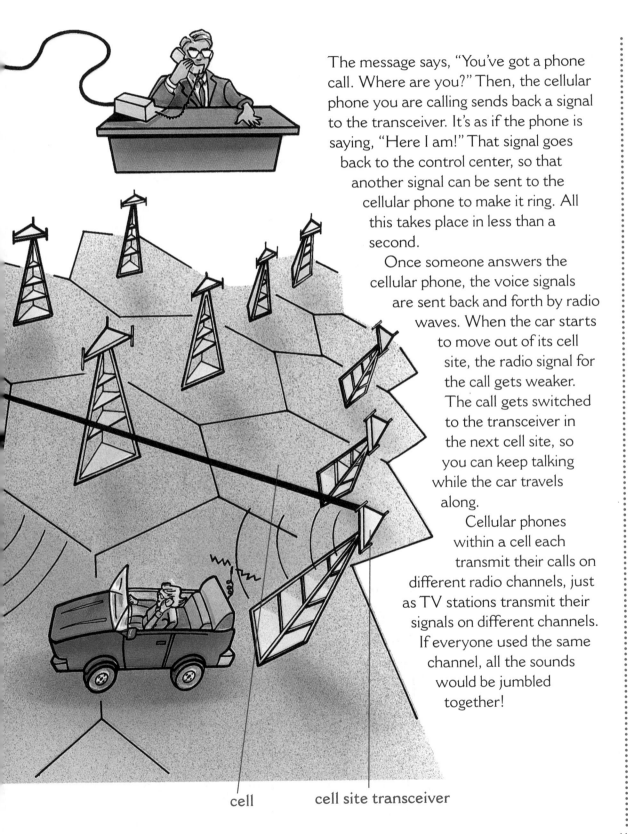

The message says, "You've got a phone call. Where are you?" Then, the cellular phone you are calling sends back a signal to the transceiver. It's as if the phone is saying, "Here I am!" That signal goes back to the control center, so that another signal can be sent to the cellular phone to make it ring. All this takes place in less than a second.

Once someone answers the cellular phone, the voice signals are sent back and forth by radio waves. When the car starts to move out of its cell site, the radio signal for the call gets weaker. The call gets switched to the transceiver in the next cell site, so you can keep talking while the car travels along.

Cellular phones within a cell each transmit their calls on different radio channels, just as TV stations transmit their signals on different channels. If everyone used the same channel, all the sounds would be jumbled together!

cell   cell site transceiver

Sometimes, cellular phones have been used for unusual purposes. Recently in California, a young man and some friends decided to stop at the bank for some cash. As they pulled into the parking lot, they saw some thieves leaving the bank with bags full of money. Driving his mother's car, the young man chased after the robbers while his friends used the car phone to call 911. Soon, a Sheriff's Department helicopter arrived on the scene. It was about time, too, since the car was almost out of gas! The young man was awarded a medal for his actions, but he admitted that chasing after the thieves might not have been such a great idea because it had put him and his friends in danger.

Cordless Telephone

A cordless telephone is a combination of a telephone and a two-way radio. It is made up of a *base phone* and a *handset*.

The base phone runs on electricity. It plugs into the wall outlet in your home. The base phone is also connected to the telephone system. It plugs into a regular phone jack.

The handset can be up to 1,500 feet from the base phone and still send and receive messages. The handset runs on batteries. The batteries are *recharged* when the handset is hung up. Recharging means to fill the batteries with energy.

A radio transmitter and receiver are built into both the base phone and the handset. The transmitter and receiver run on electricity. The person talking sends signals—his or her voice—using the transmitter. The person listening gets signals—the voice—through the receiver. An antenna on the base phone sends signals and gets signals from the antenna on the handset.

Radio signals can go through anything except metal. The cordless phone can send and receive radio signals at the same time. Callers can talk and listen at the same time. (Walkie-talkies can only do one thing at a time.)

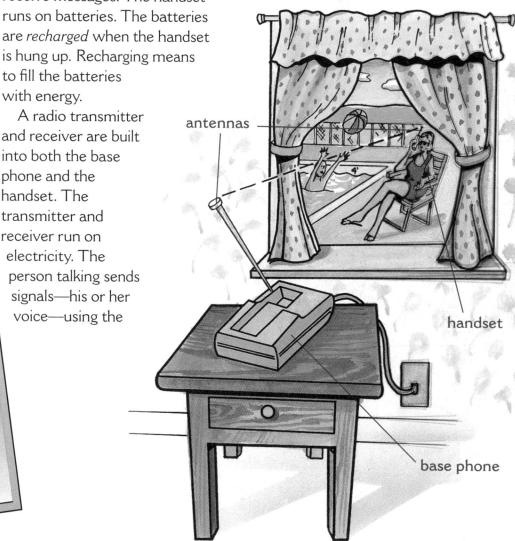

antennas

handset

base phone

A few years ago, a man from Connecticut thought he was losing his mind. All day and all night he heard music and voices in his head. The man went to a doctor, who quickly discovered the cause of the problem. The man had some dental work done, and a piece of silver had become wedged between two teeth. The silver was acting like a cordless phone and picking up radio and TV signals, which were sent through the bones of his face directly into his inner ear.

Answering Machine

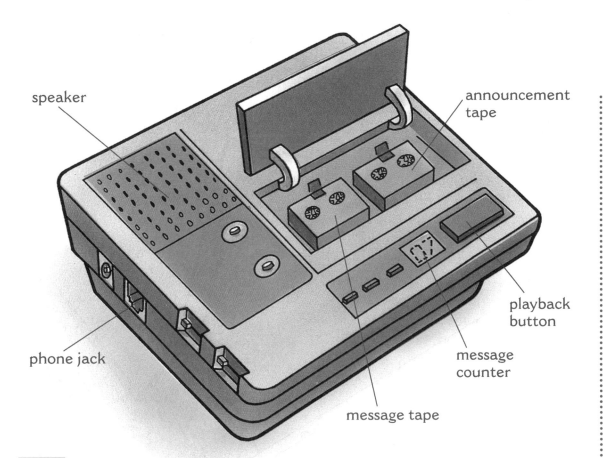

speaker

announcement tape

playback button

message counter

phone jack

message tape

Your answering machine can answer a phone call from your friend while you're away. It records your friend's voice, so that you can hear the message when you get back home.

After your phone rings a few times and no one answers it, the answering machine takes the call. It plays an *announcement tape,* which is a recording of your voice saying something like, "Hello. I can't take your call right now. Please leave a message." Then the machine plays a beep, which tells your friend that the machine is ready to record.

Next, the machine records your friend's voice on the *message tape.* When your friend hangs up, the message tape stops recording. The machine sets itself to tape the next message that comes in. It also sends a signal to the *message counter,* increasing the number on the counter by one. The counter shows you how many messages are on the tape.

Once you get home, you can press the *playback button.* The message tape will rewind and play the message for you. The speaker makes it sound loud and clear.

With some answering machines, you can call the machine and hear your messages. To get the message tape to play, you have to tell the machine your "password," a series of numbers that you press on a push-button phone. In this way, no one else can call and listen to your messages—unless they know your password.

The audiotape player was invented in 1899 by V. Poulsen. You could almost imagine Poulsen predicted that his machine would be used along with a telephone because he called his invention the "telegraphone." The earliest models used steel tape, not plastic.

Today, many answering machines don't use tapes at all. They record the outgoing and incoming messages digitally. That means they convert sounds into a series of numbers stored in a computer.

Communications Satellite

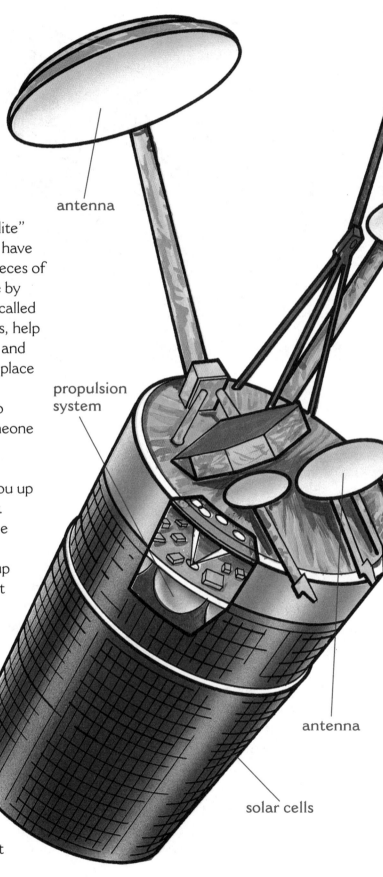

antenna

propulsion system

antenna

solar cells

A satellite is an object that *orbits,* or travels in a curved path, around another object. Did you know that the Moon is a satellite of Earth? It's true, but we usually use the word "satellite" to describe objects that people have built. These satellites are big pieces of equipment launched into space by rockets. Some satellites, called communications satellites, help send television programs and telephone calls from one place on Earth to another.

Imagine you wanted to make a phone call to someone on the other side of the world. There are no telephone wires to link you up with a phone so far away. However, your call can be sent using radio waves. Radio signals that make up your call are sent out, but these signals travel in straight lines. They can't curve around Earth. Satellites help, acting like mirrors in the sky, bouncing your signal around the planet to reach a place far away.

Radio signals that carry the information about a phone call or a television program are first sent

The idea of using some kind of communications satellite goes back to the year 1946. At that time, American scientists suggested bouncing signals off the Moon. Ten years later they began looking into the possibility of using artificial satellites. Only seven years after that, the first one was launched.

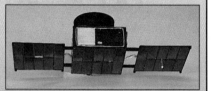

This tiny communications satellite was nicknamed "Bitsy" by its makers.

to a satellite from a *ground station*. An antenna on the satellite receives the signal. Then the signals are made stronger, and another antenna beams the signals back to Earth. On Earth, a *satellite dish* collects the beam of radio signals. The dish focuses the beam on its antenna, which picks up the signals. Telephone and television companies use these signals, changing them back to the sound or picture information that was sent at the start.

Many communications satellites orbit Earth 22,300 feet up. A satellite's speed is the same as the speed the planet turns, so the satellite stays over the same spot on Earth's surface. Many satellites are in orbit, so every place on Earth has a satellite overhead to send signals to.

The satellite's *propulsion system* helps it hold its position by making very small changes in its speed. The satellite is covered with *solar cells,* which change sunlight into electricity to power the satellite. Some electricity is stored in batteries, so the satellite will have power when it is on the dark side of Earth.

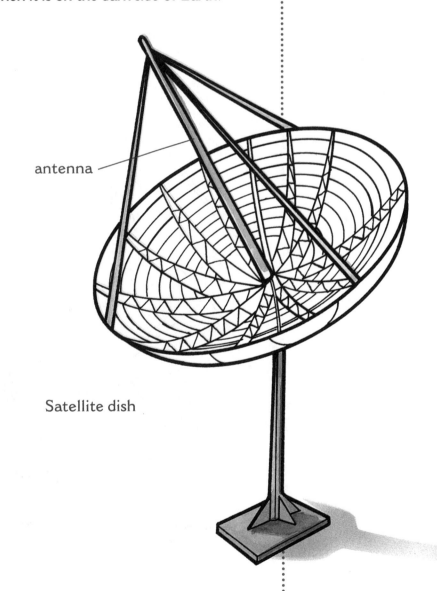

antenna

Satellite dish

Fax Machine

Sending a typed page, a handwritten note, a photo, or a drawing is easy, using a fax machine. The word "fax" is short for *facsimile,* which means "an exact copy." A fax machine sends information over the telephone lines to another fax machine. That machine produces an exact copy of the page the first machine sent.

To send a page, you feed it into the fax machine. *Rollers* grab it and move it through the machine. A *light source* shines light on the page, but only across a narrow strip at a time, the *scanning line.* That strip of light is reflected by mirrors onto a *photodetector,* a part of the machine that is sensitive to light. If you could look at the scanning line, it would look like a series of light and dark spaces. Other types of fax machines scan the pages using different kinds of lights and photodetectors, but they also scan one line at a time.

This row of light and dark spaces is changed into a series of on/off signals, which is sent to a *modem* (see

Fax machine sending a page

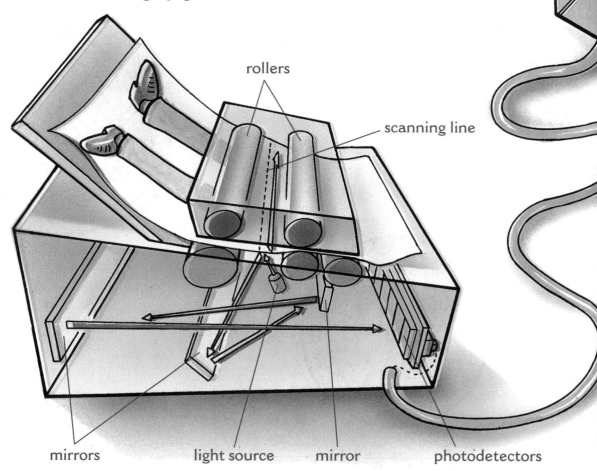

rollers

scanning line

mirrors   light source   mirror   photodetectors

Fax machine receiving a page

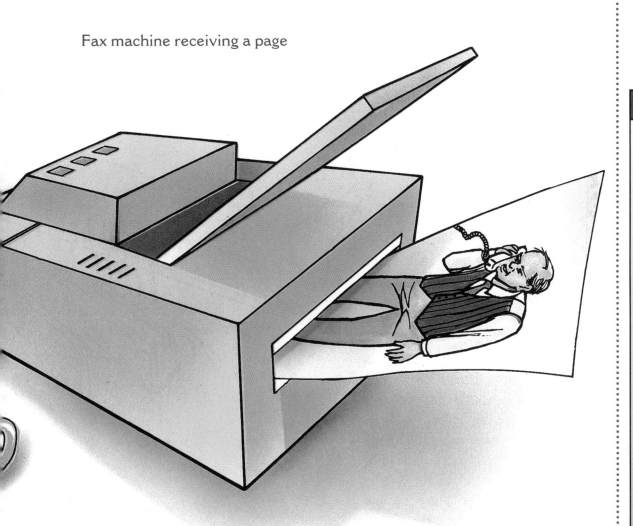

Incredibly, the history of the fax machine goes back to 1862 and an Italian priest named Abbé Caselli. In that year, Caselli invented a method of sending handwritten messages and pictures over an ordinary telegraph line. The priest succeeded only in sending blurry lines and shadows, but his basic ideas were the same as those used in making the modern fax machine.

Fax transmissions today are much clearer than that first attempt.

page 127). The modem is a device that plugs into your phone line and is built into your fax machine. The modem changes the signals so they can be sent over the telephone lines to the other fax machine.

Line by line, the page you are sending is changed into signals, until the whole page has been scanned. Then, line by line, the other fax machine uses the signals to print a series of light and dark spaces for each line. The receiving fax machine puts all the lines of light and dark back together to make a copy of the original page.

Millions of people all over the world use fax machines. Some fax machines can be programmed to send the same page to a hundred or more different places! That's a lot easier—and faster—than printing, folding, stuffing, and stamping a hundred letters!

Photocopier

How does a photocopying machine make copies?

1. The page to be copied is placed facedown on the glass window.

2. Bright lights sweep across the image on the page.

3. Mirrors reflect the light from the image onto a drum.

4. The drum is coated with a special material, a *photoconductor*. A photoconductor conducts electricity—it helps electricity flow— when the light shines on it.

5. The drum turns against a *corona*. A corona gives the drum a positive electric charge. (The positive charges are shown here by the "+" signs.)

6. Wherever the reflected image is dark, the drum has a positive charge. Wherever the reflected image is light, it causes the positive charge to disappear. The charge is now the exact shape of the letters and pictures.

7. The *toner* is given a negative charge. (The negative charges are shown here as tiny circles.) The toner is a black chemical powder. Just as with a magnet, the negative charge is *attracted* to the positive charge. The negative charge goes toward the

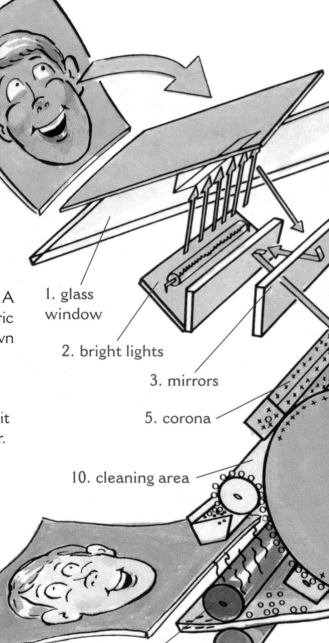

1. glass window

2. bright lights

3. mirrors

5. corona

10. cleaning area

11. copy

9. hot rollers

positive charge. The toner is attracted to parts of the drum that have the positive charge, which are the dark parts of the image being copied.

8. To get the toner to leave the drum and stick to the paper, the paper is given a positive charge by another corona. The positive charge given to the paper is stronger than the positive charge given to the drum. The toner powder is attracted off the drum and onto the paper.

9. The paper passes through two hot rollers. The heat melts the toner powder. The rollers turn the black powder image into an image that will not rub off the paper.

10. The drum must roll to a cleaning area after every copy the machine makes. Old toner is cleaned off so that new toner can be put on for another copy. This happens in less than a second.

11. The copy slides out of the machine. You may have trouble telling the copy from the original!

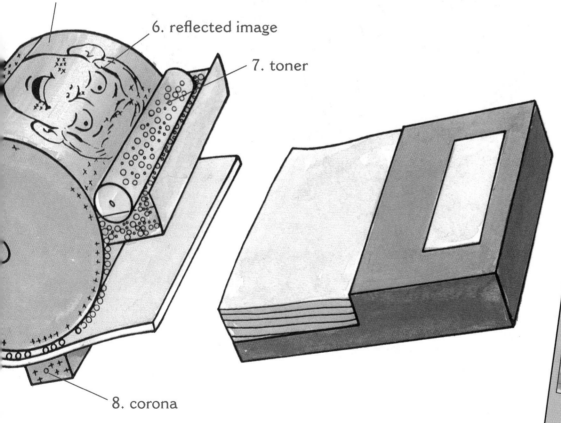

4. drum

6. reflected image

7. toner

8. corona

Chester Carlson invented the photocopier in 1938. He was certain he had come up with something fantastic. Carlson went from company to company trying to get them interested in manufacturing his machine in large numbers. Incredibly, no one was interested! Ten years passed. Finally, Carlson demonstrated his photocopier for a small family-owned firm, the Haloid Company. They were impressed. Today the Haloid Company is the huge Xerox Corporation.

Chester Carlson with his invention.

Personal Computer

software

monitor

CPU

disk drives

floppy disks

printer

mouse

keyboard

A personal computer (PC) has many parts to it. It has a "brain"—the *central processing unit* (CPU). And it has other machine parts that help you give information to the CPU and get information back. These parts include the keyboard, the mouse, the monitor, the disk drives, the printer, and the software. With all its parts working together, the PC uses and stores information.

To use the computer, you need a way to "talk" with it. The *keyboard* sends signals to the CPU. Pressing a key on a computer keyboard sends a signal to the CPU. The CPU can tell which key was pressed. Some keys type letters and numbers. Others give different commands. They tell the computer to do something such as erase, add a word, or print.

A computer system also needs a way to "talk" back to the user. A video screen *displays* (shows) words, numbers, and—on some computers—pictures. The computer's screen is called a *monitor,* and it works like your television set. The monitor shows you what you've written or drawn.

Some computers have a *mouse.* The mouse, like the keyboard, sends its own signals to the computer. Rolling the mouse over a flat surface moves the *cursor.* The cursor is the blinking line or square on the monitor's screen. It tells you where you are on the screen. Once the cursor is in place, you can perform actions on the screen by pressing one or more buttons on the mouse. Different computer programs use the mouse differently.

Computers can deal with a huge amount of information. Some of the information is the program that works the computer. Some of the information is the work you have done. Either way, the information is stored so the computer can use it.

Information is stored in the computer's *hard drive* or on *floppy disks.* Floppy disks are magnetic disks enclosed in square plastic envelopes. The disks can be filled with information much the same way a tape cassette holds music. They slip inside the computer's *disk drives.* A disk drive reads the information on the floppy disk. Many computers have at least one drive for floppy disks and a built-in hard drive. The hard drive can store much more information than a floppy disk.

The computer also can print information on paper if it is connected to a *printer.* The printer changes signals from the CPU into *characters.* Characters are the symbols—letters, numbers, or pictures—that appear on the keyboard. Some printers print in a dot pattern. The dots are arranged to look like the characters. Other printers spray ink onto the paper to form characters, while others work like a photocopier. A printer can make changes in the size and shape of the characters, and it can print pictures.

A computer system can be used for writing, drawing, or lots of other things. It can help you figure out a math problem or it can play a game with you. But it needs programs to tell it how to do these things. These programs are called *software.*

The first computer programmer was a noblewoman who lived in the 1800s, Lady Augusta Ada Lovelace. She invented a program for what was then called the "analytical engine." This machine never actually worked, but its principles were later used to develop today's computers. In 1982, the United States Department of Defense honored her work by naming a new computer language "Ada."

Lady Augusta Ada Lovelace

125

Computer Peripherals

Your computer might have another peripheral called a *mouse.* It is a little box-shaped gadget with a wire that attaches to the computer. It looks something like a mouse with a tail! You can use the mouse to enter information into the computer. Inside the mouse is a ball. As you move the mouse across your desktop, the ball rolls, which causes an arrow on the computer screen to move in the same direction. You move the arrow until it stops on an *icon,* a tiny picture on the screen that stands for a job the computer can do. Then you click a button on the mouse, and the computer will do the job you chose.

dot matrix printer

The word "peripheral" means "around the outside edge." Computer peripherals are pieces of equipment that are outside the computer itself. People use computer peripherals to put information or programs into the computer, or to get information back from the computer.

Imagine you are typing a story into a computer. One peripheral you need is the *keyboard,* which has letter and number buttons for you to press. Another is the *monitor,* or *video display terminal* (VDT). It looks like a television set. The screen on the monitor shows you the words you have typed.

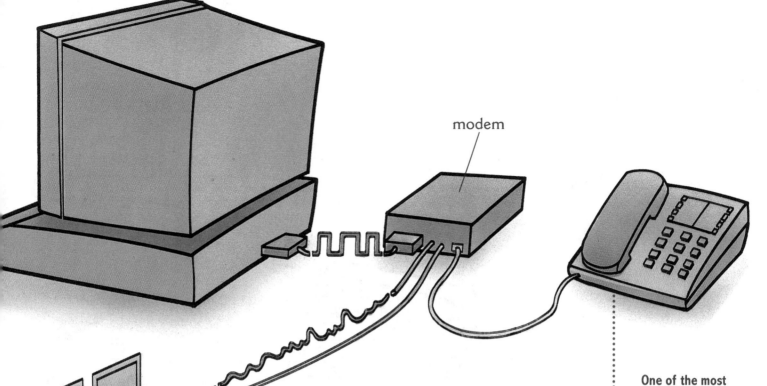

modem

icon

mouse

roller

Once you have finished your story, you can print it on paper using a *printer*. You might use a dot matrix printer or a laser printer. A dot matrix printer uses metal pins to strike a ribbon against the paper. Each pin marks a dot, and the patterns made by the dots form letters, numbers, or pictures on your paper. A laser printer works like a photocopier (see pages 122-123), except that it uses information from the computer rather than an original copy.

You could send a copy of your story to a friend using another peripheral, a *modem*. This device connects your computer with the telephone system. It changes the signals from your computer so they can travel across telephone lines. People can use modems to communicate with other computers. They can send *e-mail* (electronic mail) messages, get information from businesses and libraries, and even connect to the *Internet*. The Internet is a network of computer users all over the world whose computers can send information to each other.

One of the most important things for farmers is to know where to put fertilizer. In the past, soil samples had to be taken from all over the fields to determine which areas needed more fertilizer. But soon, farmers will be using satellite-linked computers to do this job a thousand times better and faster. Scientists are now working on an exciting new computer peripheral. It is a computerized sensor that attaches to the front of a tractor. The sensor continuously tests the soil as the tractor drives along, telling the farmer how much fertilizer to release.

Calculator

A calculator is like a tiny computer. It can do math problems *automatically*, or on its own.

Inside the calculator is a *microchip*. A microchip is a very small electronic device. Thousands of parts may be connected to the microchip. These parts are connected in *circuits*. (A circuit is a loop.) When you press the keys of a calculator, you are controlling some of the circuits on the microchip. You are sending on/off signals to the circuits that do the math problem—addition, subtraction, and so on.

Because we have ten fingers, people began counting in groups of ten. We call this kind of counting the *decimal* system. "Deci" comes from the Latin word for "ten." The circuits in a calculator can be only "on" or "off." This system of two choices is a *binary* system. "Bi" comes from the Latin word for "two." A "1" means the circuit is "on." A "0" means the circuit is "off." Any number can be written as a binary number.

When you push buttons on a calculator, the calculator transforms the numbers you enter into the binary system. The numbers become patterns of on/off signals. The calculator does math with these binary numbers.

To give you your answer, the calculator changes numbers from binary code into numbers you can read. To do this, circuits change the binary numbers into signals. The signals make some parts of the display screen darker.

Each space on the screen has seven short lines on it. These seven lines go in different directions. A number can be formed by showing only some of the lines. The number eight is the only number that is made of all the lines.

Look at the number five that is shown. When a signal is sent to one of the seven lines, that line is made dark. The rest of the display stays light. Your answer looks like dark "printing" on the screen. The part of the display screen that receives no signal stays light. The part that does receive a signal turns dark. When the right parts are dark, you have your answer.

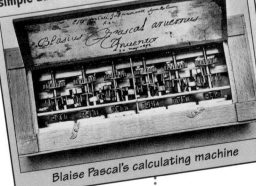

The calculator was invented in 1642 by a 19-year-old French boy named Blaise Pascal. Pascal came up with his invention to help his father, a clerk. Pascal's father had to do a huge number of mathematical calculations every day for his job. The teenager's invention consisted of a wooden box with 16 dials on it. By turning the dials, one could do simple addition and subtraction very quickly.

Blaise Pascal's calculating machine

Robot

Robots are all around us, and most don't look human at all. A robot is really a computer with an attachment—such as an "arm"—that lets it work.

One type of robot is simply a metal "arm," "wrist," and "hand." The robot can reach, grab, and turn to do a job. For instance, a robot arm can be made to tighten bolts in car engines. The hand may be a wrench that fits onto the bolts. The arm reaches out until the wrench fits onto a bolt. The wrist turns to tighten the bolt.

Valves make the arm, wrist, and hand work, and a computer controls the valves. (Valves are tubes that control the flow of a gas or liquid.) The valves let oil flow through different parts of the arm,

wrist, or hand. The pressure of the flowing oil makes the parts move. This is called a *hydraulic system*.

The valves are controlled by the computer. The computer uses a *feedback system* to move the valves. The computer, for example, tells the arm where to move. A signal tells the computer when the arm has moved there. The computer then sends signals to the arm to go on to the next step.

During the World's Fair of 1939-1940, the Westinghouse Company exhibited Elektro, the Mechanical Man. The 7-foot, 260-pound robot was set in motion by the vibrations of the human voice. Elektro could walk, count on his fingers up to ten, tell the color of an object held in front of him, and perform twenty other tricks. The robot's electrical system contained 24,900 miles of wire—enough to wrap all the way around Earth.

Electro with his mechanical pet

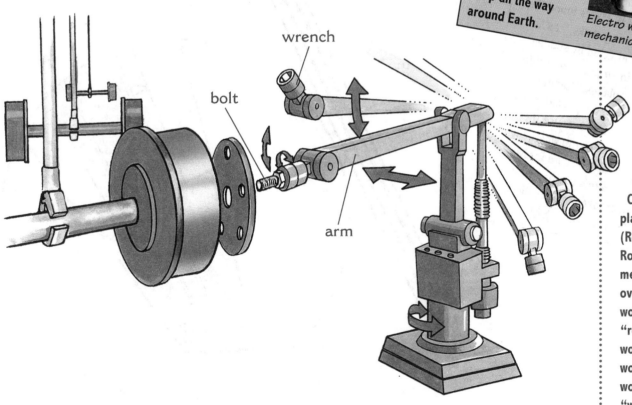

wrench

bolt

arm

The word "robot" became familiar in 1920, when Karel Capek of Czechoslovakia wrote a play called *R.U.R.* (Rossum's Universal Robots). In the play, mechanical workers take over the world. These workers are called "robots"—the same word we use today. The word comes from a Czech word, *robota*, that means "work."

Pen

A pen writes by putting ink onto paper. The ink dries very fast. A common pen is the ballpoint pen. A plastic *casing* holds the ballpoint pen together. Ink flows through a tube inside the casing. One end of the tube is a *socket*. The socket holds a tiny rolling ball. As the ball rolls, it becomes coated with ink. The ink is then rolled onto the paper.

Quill pens of long ago were made of goose, swan, or crow feathers. The inside core of these feathers was hollow. The core could hold a little ink. The feather tip was split and carved to a point. Ink would flow from inside the feather to the tip. The tip scratched ink against the paper. The quill was dipped into an inkwell to soak up more ink into its core. The fountain pen is the modern form of a quill pen. Fountain pens have a supply of ink inside them, so that you don't have to keep dipping the tip into an inkwell.

A felt-tipped pen is a cross between a fountain pen and a paintbrush. The felt tip is soaked with ink that is like a fast-drying paint. When the felt tip rubs against the paper, it "paints" a line.

In the 1930s, a Hungarian chemist named Ladislao Biro was getting fed up with his old-fashioned fountain pen. Fiddling around in his workshop, Biro came up with the idea of putting printer's ink inside a pen. For the pen's tip, he made a little ball that picked up more ink as it rolled. Biro's pens were first used in large numbers by the Allied Air Force during World War II. Flyers found that Biro's "non-leaking writing sticks," as he called them, were not affected by sudden changes in air pressure inside their planes. Mountain climbers liked them, too, because they can write where the air pressure is low. Biro's company was later taken over by Bic, a French company.

casing

ink

tube

socket

ball

Air Bag

The air bag works if the car hits something or is hit.

1. The air bag pops out only in a crash that happens at 12 miles per hour or more. Even at 12 miles per hour—not very fast for a car—the driver can be hurt. An air bag works *automatically*—it works on its own. The driver does nothing to make it work.

2. An air bag is like a big balloon. The cloth bag is kept in the center of the steering wheel. The crash sends a signal to the air bag. The air bag *inflates,* or blows up, faster than the blink of an eye. The air bag is filled with gas in less than a second. The gas is harmless.

3. The air bag protects the driver in a crash. Instead of the driver hitting his or her head against a hard steering wheel, the driver hits a soft air bag.

4. Once it has done its job, the air bag *deflates,* or flattens, in another blink of an eye. The gas escapes through openings in the cloth bag.

An air bag has been invented for bicycle riders. It is inside the cyclist's helmet. Upon sudden contact, the bag inflates. It creates a cushion for the skull, and a rounded neck-piece opens up to protect the spine. Nobody knows yet when this invention might be available in stores.

Even without air bags, a bicycle safety helmet can help protect you from injuries and should always be worn when you go cycling.

Car

muffler

drum brake

spring

differential

fuel tank

A car has many parts. The engine is the part that changes energy into the power to turn the car's wheels. The engine gets its power by burning gasoline, which is stored in the fuel tank. Since the engine heats up as it runs, the *radiator* is needed to cool it down.

A car works like a bicycle, where one set of wheels is powered and the other wheels just roll along. In rear-wheel drive cars, the rear wheels get the power. The engine's power is passed along through the *transmission,* the *drive shaft,* and the *differential* to the back wheels.

The transmission switches the gears that turn the wheels, making the wheels turn fast or slow. The drive shaft connects the transmission to the differential. When the car goes around corners, the differential lets the wheel on one side of the car turn at a different speed from the wheel on the other side. Without the differential, the car could skid on turns.

In front-wheel drive cars, the engine powers the front wheels. The engine, transmission, and differential are put together in a unit called a *transaxle.*

Many cars have *disc brakes* on the front wheels and *drum brakes* in back. In both kinds of brakes, part of the brake spins with the wheel. Another part pushes against it to slow the wheel down.

Many other parts connect to the engine. The *exhaust manifold* carries away the exhaust, or waste gases, from the engine. The exhaust travels through a pipe to the *catalytic converter,* which removes harmful gases. The exhaust also passes through a *muffler,* which absorbs some of the engine's noise.

The 1863 Lenoir was the first car. Invented by J.J. Etienne Lenoir, it was also the first in a long line of cars named for their builders. Ranson E. Olds, who started the Olds Motor Vehicle Company in 1897, named the Oldsmobile after himself. David Buick, Louis Chevrolet, Henry Ford, Walter P. Chrysler, Ferdinand Porsche, and brothers John and Horace Dodge also immortalized their names with their cars. Perhaps most interesting of all is the Mercedes-Benz. Benz was the name of Karl Benz, the German pioneer in gas engines and motor-driven vehicles. Mercedes was the first name of a little girl, Mercedes Jellinek, whose father invested a great deal of money in the Benz company.

An 1888 Mercedes-Benz

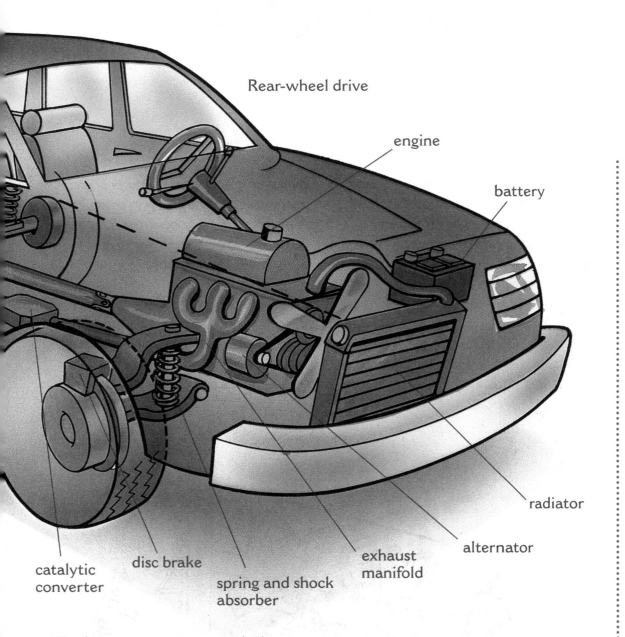

Rear-wheel drive

engine

battery

radiator

alternator

catalytic
converter

disc brake

spring and shock
absorber

exhaust
manifold

The *battery* stores energy, which you
need to start the car and power the
lights. Like any battery, this battery can
wear out. To keep it running, the
alternator gets power from the engine to
produce electricity. This electricity
recharges the battery.

Springs and *shock absorbers* connect
the wheel's axles to the body of the car.
They keep the car riding smoothly when
it goes over bumps. The springs take up
some of the force when the car hits a
bump. The shock absorbers slow down
the springs to keep them from making
the car bounce.

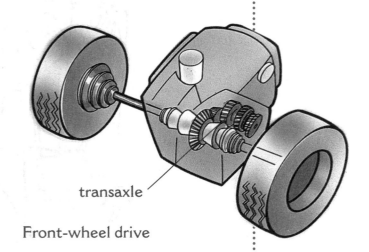

transaxle

Front-wheel drive

Gasoline Engine

Inside a gasoline engine, one tiny explosion after another takes place, over and over again. These explosions provide the power to turn the wheels of a car.

Many cars have four *cylinders*—wide, round tubes—where the explosions take place. An *intake valve* lets a mixture of air and gasoline into each cylinder. A *spark plug* makes a spark, which causes the air and gasoline mixture to explode.

Every time an explosion takes place, it pushes against the *piston* in the cylinder. A piston is like a stopper that can move up and down. Then, an *exhaust valve* lets the leftover gases escape from the cylinder.

A *connecting rod* links each piston with the crankshaft, a series of connected pieces that turn. As the pistons move up and down, they turn the crankshaft, which moves the *drive belt*. This belt

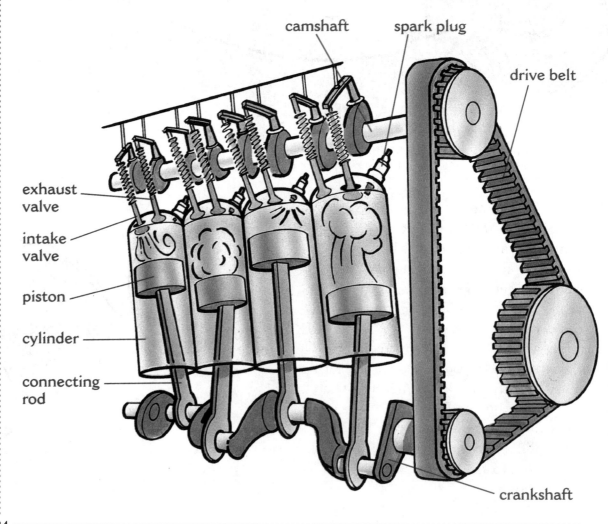

camshaft   spark plug   drive belt

exhaust valve

intake valve

piston

cylinder

connecting rod

crankshaft

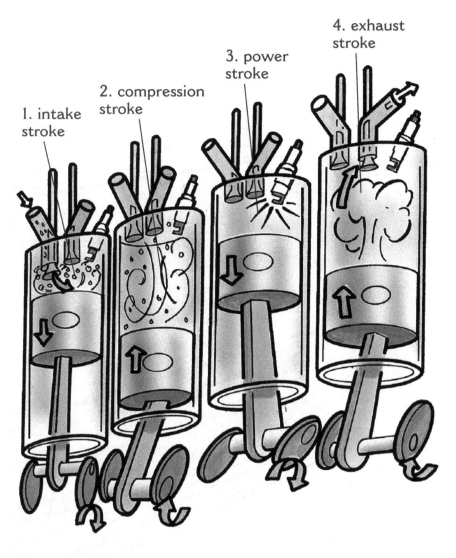

1. intake stroke

2. compression stroke

3. power stroke

4. exhaust stroke

connects to other parts of the car that end up turning the wheels. The drive belt also turns the *camshaft*, which controls when the valves open and close.

For all these parts to work, the explosions have to be timed just right. The pistons have to go up and down in just the right order to make the crankshaft turn smoothly. Each piston repeats four *strokes*, or movements. The whole cycle of four strokes takes less than a second.

1. First, the intake valve opens and the piston moves down, drawing the air and gasoline mixture into the cylinder. This is the *intake stroke*.

2. Next, the piston moves back up again. It *compresses*, or squeezes, the air and gasoline mixture into a small space. This is the *compression stroke*.

3. Now, the spark plug fires off a spark. The mixture explodes and forces the piston down. This is the *power stroke*.

4. The exhaust valve opens and the piston moves up. The exhaust, or waste gas, is pushed out of the cylinder. This is the *exhaust stroke*.

The world is running out of gasoline, and scientists are looking for a new type of fuel. The answer may be in peanuts! One day a man in Oklahoma had an idea. He poured peanut oil into his gas tank, and the car ran just as well as ever. Some scientists are now considering peanut oil as a possible replacement for gasoline. You won't be seeing peanut oil at gas stations any time soon, though. It seems peanut oil can really clog up some engine parts and harm the engine.

Subway Train

Subway trains run on electricity. Most subway tracks have two main rails on which the train rolls. A third rail is the electric rail. The third rail can be between the main tracks or off to one side. It carries 500 to 700 volts of electricity—much more powerful than the electricity running through your home.

Electricity travels through a *circuit,* or loop. The circuit in a subway train goes from the tracks to the cars and back again.

To get from the track to the train, electricity flows through a *conducting shoe,* a piece of metal that touches the third rail. From the conducting shoe, electricity flows to the train's motors, lights, and doors. Electricity also runs the train's heating and air-conditioning systems.

The train's motors sit inside its *trucks.* The trucks hold the *axles.* An axle is a rod that has a wheel on each end. The train's wheels are made of steel. The wheels *conduct,* or move, electricity out of the train and back to the main tracks. The circuit is complete.

The driver controls the train with a *lever.* Pushing the lever forward sends the train forward. Letting the lever move back into place slows and stops the train.

Subway cars can be added to the train if the train has to carry a lot of people. Subway cars can be removed from the train if there are only a few people to carry. In the morning, a dozen cars may be hooked together by a *hitch.* Late at night, a car may run alone.

hitch

lever

conducting shoe

The first subway was built in London in 1863 and was only four miles long. When they first had the idea many years earlier, the planners discussed whether to use trains or horse-drawn carriages. They finally decided on small trains. When the subway opened for operation, there were six engines, each pulling four cars. The passenger compartments were lit with gas lamps.

A London subway station in the 1890s

air vent to
street level

truck

axle

main rails

electric rail

Maglev

A "maglev" is a "magnetically levitated train." *Magnetically* means "with a magnet." *Levitate* means "to rise" or "to float." A magnetically levitated train is a train that uses a magnet to rise off a track.

A maglev runs on a *guideway*. Guideways are tracks made of concrete and steel. The guideways are lined with *electromagnets*. The electromagnet has a core, or center, of metal. Wire is wound around the core. Electricity running through the wire turns the core into a magnet. Electromagnets can be very powerful. The electromagnets on the guideway *repel*—or push away from— the electromagnets on the train, lifting the train off the guideway.

The *flange* on each side of the maglev wraps around the guideway. The flange is the bottom of the train. Electromagnets line the inside of each flange. The magnets on the track pull the lower lip of the flange toward the guideway.

A computer measures the distance between the electromagnets and the guideway. The strength of the *magnetic repulsion*, the force of the electromagnets repelling each other, must be the same all along the guideway.

Alignment magnets are placed inside the sides of the flange. They keep the train running straight along the guideway.

The magnets along the side of the guideway

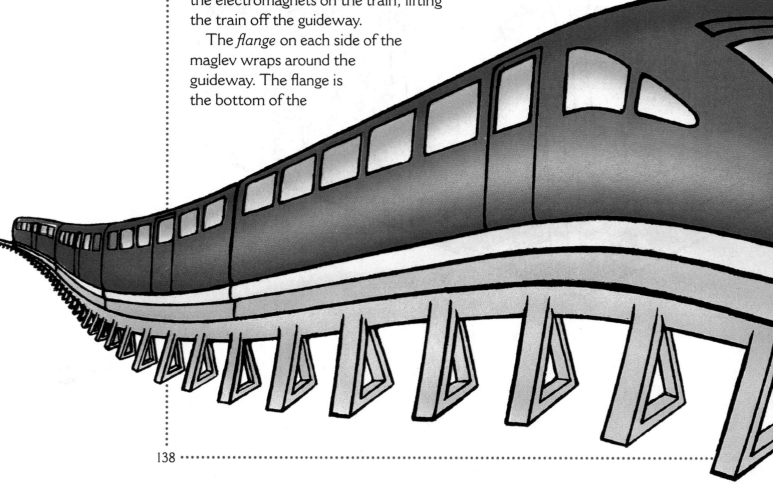

pull the train forward. The electricity that runs through the guideway's electromagnets flows very fast. As the electricity flows through each magnet along the guideway, that magnet pulls the train toward it. As the magnets pull the train, the train makes its way down the guideway.

Because the maglev train rides in the air, there is no *friction* between the train and the guideway. Friction is the force created when objects rub against each other or when an object rubs against the air. Friction between a normal train's wheels and the track slows the train down. Trains also have to work against air resistance—the friction between the train and the air it moves through. With only air resistance to work against, the maglev can travel at very high speeds. Some models have reached 275 to 300 miles per hour!

alignment magnets

flange

electromagnets

guideway

In the 1830s, Dr. Dionysius Lardner, a highly respected English scientist, made a prediction. Dr. Lardner said that trains would never be able to travel at high speeds, such as 100 miles per hour. If they did, he concluded, the passengers would be unable to breathe and would die of suffocation. If Dr. Lardner were alive today, he would surely be shocked to see a maglev shoot past at 250 to 300 miles per hour!

Skateboard

A skateboard, or deck, is a board with two *axles*. An axle is a rod with a wheel on each end. *Trucks* attach the axles to the board. The trucks are T-shaped metal pieces that let the rider steer.

When the rider presses down on one side of the board with a foot, the part of the truck that holds the axle turns a little. Because the truck turns, the wheel can turn. Each wheel spins by itself. The skateboard goes in the direction of the pressure.

The truck acts like a *hinge,* a metal piece that lets things move. (A hinge lets a swinging door swing, for example.) The truck hinges on two points. One point is the pin at one end of the truck. The other point is the ring on the other end of the truck. A *bolt* goes through the ring. (A bolt is like a short rod. A *nut* screws on the end of the bolt. A bolt and nut are used to fasten things together.) The bolt connects the ring to the truck. Thick rubber rings fit between the bolt and the ring. Making a nut looser or tighter makes turning easier.

When the rider presses down on the board, the truck and the axle bend toward the side being pressed down. When the rider lets up on the pressure, the rubber rings push the truck back into place.

If the truck were like a regular hinge, the wheels would just move toward the board when the rider pressed down on the side. Because the pin sits closer to the board than the ring sits, the truck bends toward the board and in the direction of the ring. Because the bolt faces the center of the board, the wheels under pressure move toward the center of the board. The outside wheels move toward the back of the board. The skateboard goes into a turn.

Many top skateboarders today perform spins and jumps on U-shaped wooden ramps. Their boards may have plastic rings on the T-shaped part of the truck. Plastic rings don't let the trucks move around as much as rubber rings do. To turn, the rider pushes down with his or her back foot rather than pushing down on one side of the board. The front of the board lifts off the ground. The board spins around on its back wheels. The *tail* turns up at the end so that it won't scrape the ground during kick turns.

The best skateboarders use the *rails* on the bottom of the board to turn. The rails are the handholds. To do this, the rider jumps off the ground, grabs the rails, and points the board in a new direction.

In 1987 in Los Angeles, Harriet Williams was walking down the street when a thief snatched her purse. The snatcher was a fast runner and thought he had made a clean getaway... when Williams's son Mike shot past on his skateboard and snatched back his mom's purse.

rubber or plastic ring

nut

axle

bolt

rail

truck

tail

Bicycle

Bicycles have gone through many changes over the past 100 years. Bicycles of the 1800s had their pedals attached to the front wheel. Pushing the pedals turned the front wheel. Every time the pedal made a whole circle, the front wheel turned around once.

Today's bicycles have pedals that are not attached to the front or rear wheel. The pedals are attached to the front *sprocket*. (A sprocket is a wheel with pointy teeth.) The sprocket is connected to the back wheel by a *chain drive*. Turning the pedals turns the sprocket. When the sprocket turns, it moves the chain. This makes the back wheel turn. As the back wheel turns, it moves the bicycle forward.

1. Pedaling turns the front sprocket, which pulls the chain around.

2. The chain runs around the front and rear sprockets. The chain is made of round rods linked together. The spaces between the rods match the spacing of the teeth of the sprockets.

3. The chain pulls across the top of the rear sprocket. This pulling turns the rear sprocket. The rear sprocket turns in the same direction as the front sprocket. Because the rear sprocket connects to the rear wheel, the rear wheel turns. The bicycle moves forward.

4. Your legs work best pedaling at 60 to 120 revolutions—complete circles—per minute. Bikes come in many "speeds," though. There are three-speeds, ten-speeds, even 21-speeds. Different speeds have rear sprockets of different sizes. A smaller sprocket makes the rear wheel turn faster. Pedaling is harder, though.

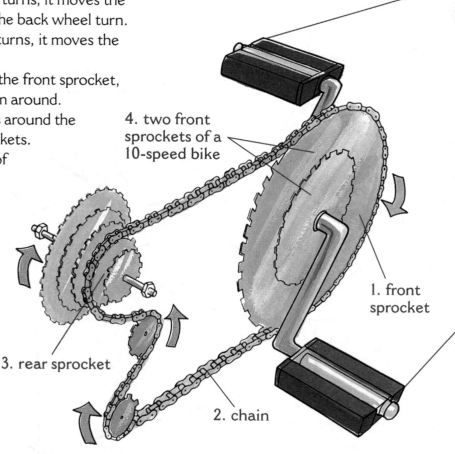

4. two front sprockets of a 10-speed bike

3. rear sprocket

2. chain

1. front sprocket

6. rear sprocket with 40 teeth

7. brake lever

5. derailleur

8. rubber shoe

9. fork

6. Every turn of a sprocket with 40 teeth pulls 40 links of chain. The rear sprocket might have only 40 teeth. As 80 links of chain pass over the rear sprocket, it turns twice. If the front sprocket has 80 teeth, one turn of the pedals produces two turns of the rear wheel.

A smaller rear sprocket might have only 20 teeth. Changing gears to this smaller sprocket means the rear wheel turns four times while the pedals turn once.

7. Levers on the handlebars operate the bike's brakes. A tug on the levers pulls the cables. The cables run to the brakes.

8. The brake is made up of a *caliper* and two rubber *shoes*. Calipers open and close like a pair of pliers. The cable pulls the two halves of the caliper together. This pushes the shoes, or rubber pads, against the wheel's rim. The turning wheel slows down. The bicycle has brakes on the front and rear wheels.

9. Turning the handlebars turns the *fork*. The fork connects to the front wheel. Turning the fork points the bike in the direction you will ride.

A ten-speed bike lets the rider choose between two front sprockets. The sprockets are different sizes.

5. To shift sprockets, or gears, the rider pulls on the shift lever. This lever pulls a cable. A cable is a rope made of wire. The cable pulls the *derailleur*. The derailleur pulls the chain onto the gear that has been chosen.

There are bicycle races in Japan to see who can go the slowest. These races are a test of balancing skills. The rider tries not to fall over while moving forward as little as possible.

Scooter

spinning wheels

The scooter was invented in 1897 by Walter Lines, a 15-year-old English schoolboy. No patent was taken out, because the boy's father did not think the invention was worthwhile. On his own, Walter went on to make scooters in large numbers and made a fortune.

Even the best scooters made today do not use chains, gears, or pedals to make them go. Their power and speed is "all in the foot."

As your foot pushes off the ground, the scooter moves forward. A few solid pushes will send the scooter off at a good speed. Once the scooter is rolling, a push now and then will keep up the speed. Going downhill is a free ride—*gravity* pulls the scooter down. Gravity is the force that pulls us to Earth. Without gravity, we would float up into the air.

The scooter's spinning wheels act like *gyroscopes*. A gyroscope spins in the same direction until *friction* slows it down. Friction is the resistance to motion created when two objects rub against each other or when an object rubs against the air. The wheels of the scooter will stand up straight as long as they are spinning fast enough. This is gyroscopic force.

To steer to the right, the rider turns the handlebars to the right. To steer left, the rider turns the handlebars left.

There are two ways to stop. The rider can put one foot down on the ground or use the scooter's *caliper brakes* (if the scooter has them). Squeezing the brake handles makes rubber brake shoes press against the rim of each wheel. As the rubber brake shoes squeeze the rim, *friction* is created. Friction makes the scooter slow down. When the scooter begins to wobble, the rider can put a foot down to come to a safe stop.

Surfboard

A surfboard rides a wave because it is *buoyant*—it can float—and because it is pulled down the slope of water by *gravity*. Gravity is the force that pulls us to Earth. Without gravity, we would float up into the air.

The trick in surfing is to slide across the wave. To surf, the surfer has to keep up with the wave. To keep up with the wave, the surfer has to match his or her speed to the wave's speed. Steering the board changes its speed. Steering downhill makes the board go faster. Steering uphill makes the board go slower.

To steer the board, the surfer leans back and lifts his or her weight off the front of the board. By shifting weight, the surfer can steer the board. To steer to the right, the surfer leans to the right and moves his or her weight backward. Because the *nose* of the board has little weight on it, it turns to the right. The *skeg* keeps the *tail* moving straight. The skeg is a fin on the bottom of the board. Without a skeg, a surfboard would skid sideways down a wave.

A coating on top of the board stops the surfer's feet from slipping. A leash, which goes around the ankle, keeps the board from drifting away when the surfer falls into the water.

A surfer once rode a 50-foot-high wave! It happened in 1868. The man was out surfing on a wooden board when, to his horror, he saw a tidal wave coming! With no other choice, he tried to ride the wave to keep from being killed by it. Amazingly, he suffered only minor injuries.

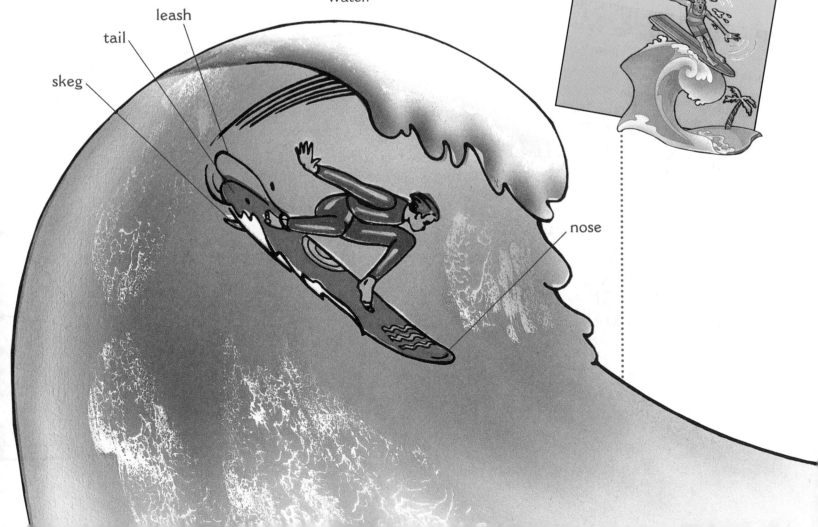

leash

tail

skeg

nose

Sailboard

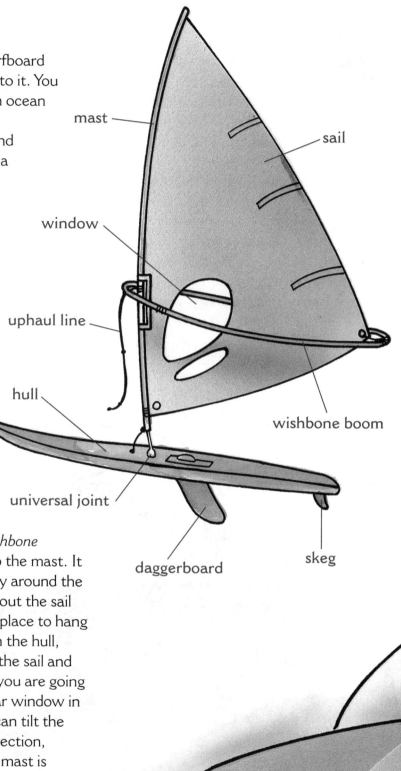

mast

sail

window

uphaul line

hull

wishbone boom

universal joint

daggerboard

skeg

A sailboard is like a surfboard with a sail attached to it. You can only ride a surfboard on ocean waves, but you can use a sailboard on lakes, ponds, and rivers—as long as you have a little wind.

The board itself is called the *hull*. It has a small fin, called a *skeg*, pointing down at the back. Another, larger fin, the *daggerboard*, points down from the center of the hull. These fins help keep the sailboard from shifting sideways as it sails.

The *mast* is a post that stands upright in the center of the hull, holding up the sail. A curved rod, called the *wishbone boom*, attaches to the mast. It curves all the way around the sail. It stretches out the sail and gives you a place to hang on. Standing on the hull, you can move the sail and watch where you are going through a clear window in the sail. You can tilt the sail in any direction, because the mast is attached to the hull by a *universal joint*, a swivel

The people of Hawaii were using sailboards long before they were "invented" in the 1960s. When English sea captain James Cook first visited the islands in 1778, he found the people there using sailboards both for sport and travel. They were heavy wooden surfboards with sails made of woven mats.

On a later trip to Hawaii, Cook was killed during a fight with a group of native people.

connection that is like your shoulder joint. If the sail falls, you can pull it back up using the *uphaul line*.

You steer a sailboard by tilting the sail in different directions. Imagine that the wind is coming from the left side of the sailboard. If you tilt the sail forward, more of the sail is toward the front of the board. As a result, the front of the board gets more of a push. The sailboard turns, moving in the same direction that the wind is blowing.

If you tilt the sail backward, more of the sail is toward the back of the board. Now the back end gets the bigger push, and the board turns in the direction that is facing the wind.

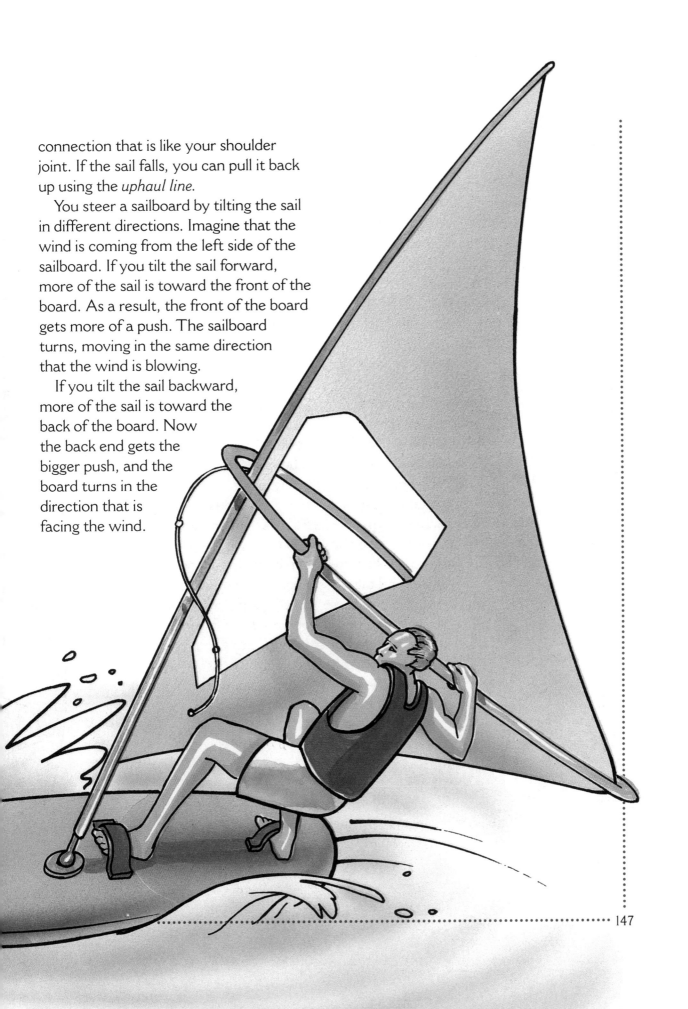

Hydrofoil

A hydrofoil is a special kind of boat that can move very fast by lifting itself up out of the water. It's almost like a boat that flies!

When any boat moves through the water, its *hull,* the bottom surface of the boat, drags against the water. This slows the boat down. The boat also makes waves. One wave is produced by the *bow,* the front of the boat. The back end of the boat, called the *stern,* makes another wave.

When a boat is moving very slowly, the bow and stern waves are both short and narrow, so they don't bump into each other very much. But when the boat speeds up, the waves become longer and taller. Soon, the boat is traveling so fast, the high point of the bow wave meets the low point of the stern wave. When this happens, the water becomes churned up. The churning water acts like a brake on the boat, slowing it down. Trying to speed up the boat only makes matters worse.

A hydrofoil gets around this problem by moving itself up, out of the way of the waves. Underneath the hull are several *foils.* The foils are surfaces shaped like airplane wings. (See pages 162-163.) When the hydrofoil is moving at high speed, the foils act like airplane wings, creating lift as the water moves over the curved top of the foils. Lift moves the foils up, raising the hull out of the water. The boat travels on the surface of the water. It rides the foils just like water skiers skim along on the water's surface on their skis. The hydrofoil can really move, clipping along at speeds of 45 to 75 miles per hour.

The power for a hydrofoil can come from a propeller engine below the surface of the water. Some hydrofoils are powered by jet pumps. They take in water and thrust it out behind the boat with great force, sending the hydrofoil forward.

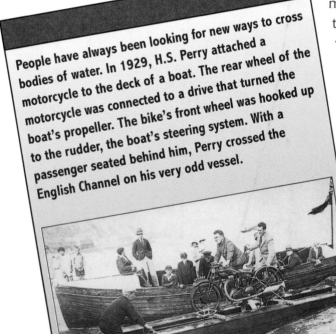

People have always been looking for new ways to cross bodies of water. In 1929, H.S. Perry attached a motorcycle to the deck of a boat. The rear wheel of the motorcycle was connected to a drive that turned the boat's propeller. The bike's front wheel was hooked up to the rudder, the boat's steering system. With a passenger seated behind him, Perry crossed the English Channel on his very odd vessel.

Perry's unusual craft

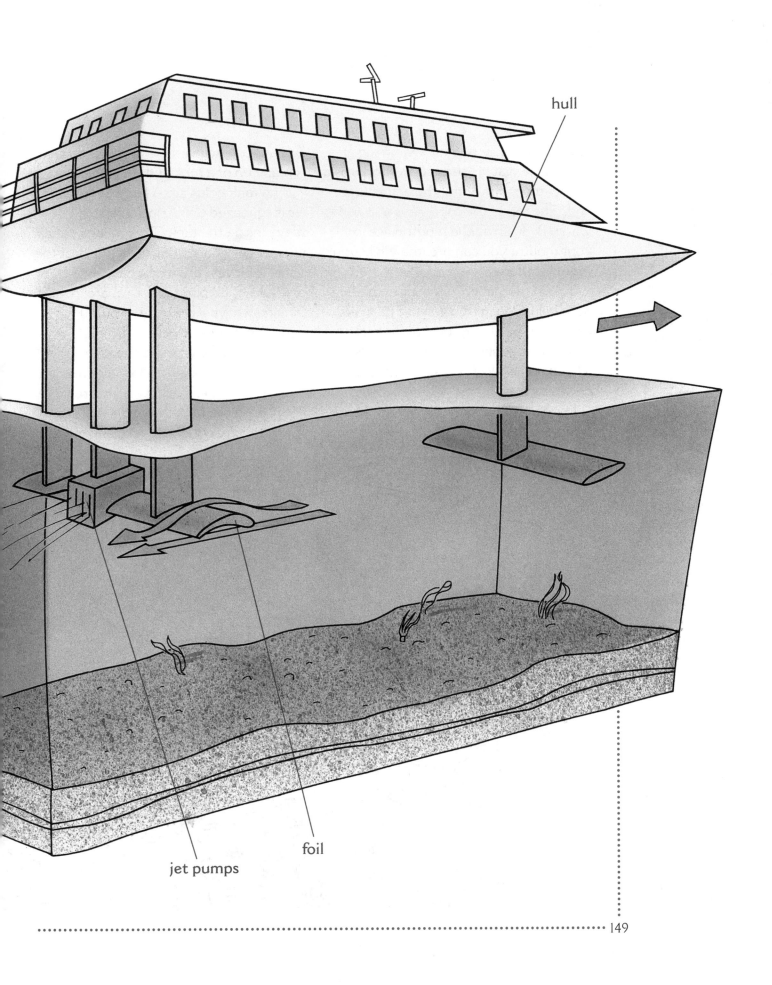

hull

foil

jet pumps

Snorkel and Scuba Gear

A snorkel is used for swimming at the water's surface. A snorkel is a hollow tube with a mouthpiece at one end. The top of the tube stays above the water. By keeping the mouthpiece in your mouth, you can breathe while you swim facedown.

The mask that covers your eyes and nose helps you in two ways. The mask helps you see clearly, because it keeps water from pushing on your eyeballs. The mask also keeps water from going up your nose.

For deeper swimming, you would use a Self-Contained Underwater Breathing Apparatus—*scuba*, for short. Scuba gear is made up of a *tank* and a *regulator*.

The tank holds air. A large amount of air is squeezed tightly into the small space inside the tank. That means the air presses very hard against the walls of the tank. A bicycle tire might have a pressure of 80 pounds per square inch. A tank may have a pressure of 3,000 pounds per square inch.

The regulator changes the high air pressure in the tank to a low air pressure you can breathe. The low-pressure air flows from the tank through a hose to the *inlet valve*. A lever opens and closes

Before scuba diving was developed, there was the diving bell. It was invented by Englishman Edmund Halley in the early 1700s. The bell was made of wood weighted with lead. It had a plate-glass window and a bench and platform for the people inside. During their stay underwater, the people in the diving bell would release spent air from a tap at the top of the bell. Fresh air was sent down in barrels encased in lead. The air was fed into the bell through leather hoses. The purpose of the diving bell was to recover sunken treasure. A man wearing a bell-shaped glass over his head would exit the bottom of the diving bell. With air fed into the glass by another leather hose, he could then walk around and search for treasure.

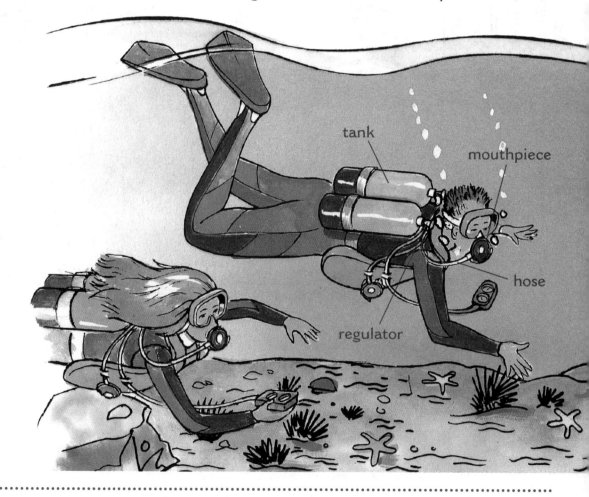

tank

mouthpiece

hose

regulator

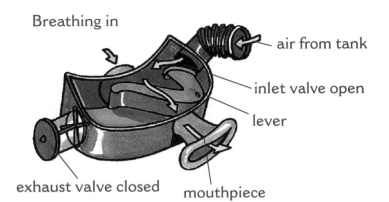

Breathing in

air from tank

inlet valve open

lever

exhaust valve closed

mouthpiece

the inlet valve. When you breathe in, the lever is sucked toward the *mouthpiece*. The inlet valve opens. Air is let in. When you stop breathing in, the lever goes back to the starting position. The inlet valve closes. When you breathe out, the inlet valve stays closed.

The pressure of your breathing opens the *exhaust valve*. The exhaust valve lets the used air out into the water. This is the stream of bubbles you see above and behind a scuba diver.

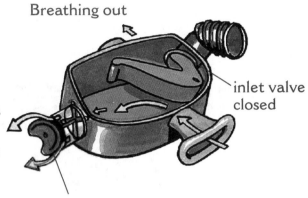

Breathing out

inlet valve closed

exhaust valve open

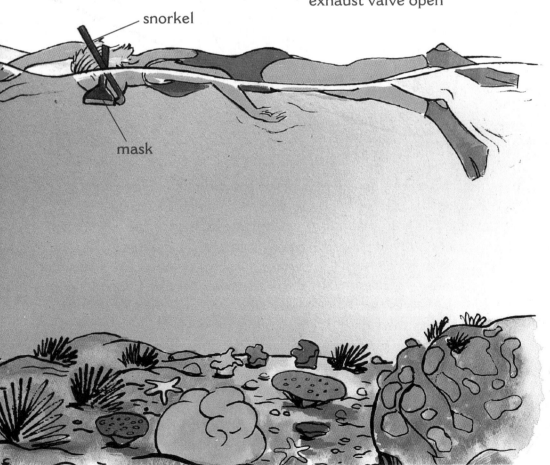

snorkel

mask

Submarine

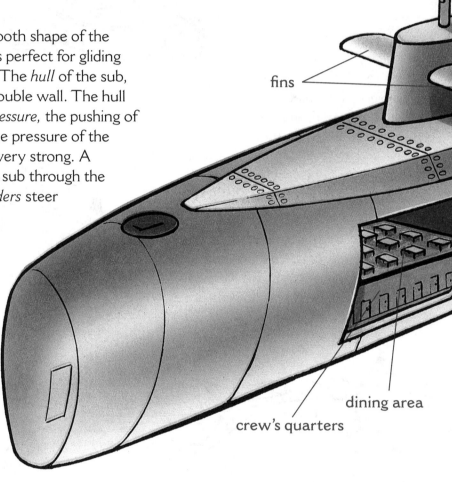

fins

dining area

crew's quarters

In 1944, an American pilot named Don Brandt was shot down during a battle to take the island of Guam. As Brandt floated near the island, the enemy blasted away at him. Suddenly he saw the periscope of an American submarine coming at him. Don grabbed hold of the periscope, tied a rope from the raft to it, and off he went, being towed along by the submarine below. After a long, bumpy, and frightening ride, the submarine stopped, several miles out to sea. Then it surfaced and Brandt was taken on board, wounded and at a total loss for words after one of the most unusual rescues in wartime history.

T he long, smooth shape of the submarine is perfect for gliding through the ocean. The *hull* of the sub, its outer skin, is a double wall. The hull stands up to high *pressure,* the pushing of water against it. The pressure of the deep water can be very strong. A *propeller* moves the sub through the water. *Fins* and *rudders* steer the submarine.

Between the double walls of the hull are *ballast chambers.* To make the sub dive, the chambers are filled with water. The water makes the submarine get heavier. As the sub gets heavier, it sinks lower—it *submerges.* To make the submarine rise, c*ompressed air* is pumped into the ballast chamber to push the water out. Compressed air is air that has been squeezed to fit into a smaller space. With more air in the ballast chambers, the submarine gets lighter, and rises.

A *conning tower* lets the crew see above the water while the sub is still underwater. This raised tower sits on top of the hull. It holds a *periscope,* radar equipment, and radio antennas. This equipment lets sailors know where they are and where they are going. The periscope actually lets the crew look

outside the submarine. The conning tower is a command center.

A nuclear submarine runs on *nuclear power* from a nuclear reactor. The *nuclear reactor* creates steam. The steam turns the *power turbine.* The turbine makes the generators run. The generators make electricity.

Electricity does many things on a submarine. It takes oxygen from sea water for the sailors to breathe. It runs the lights in the dining area and the crew's quarters. Electricity also runs the motor that makes the propeller spin.

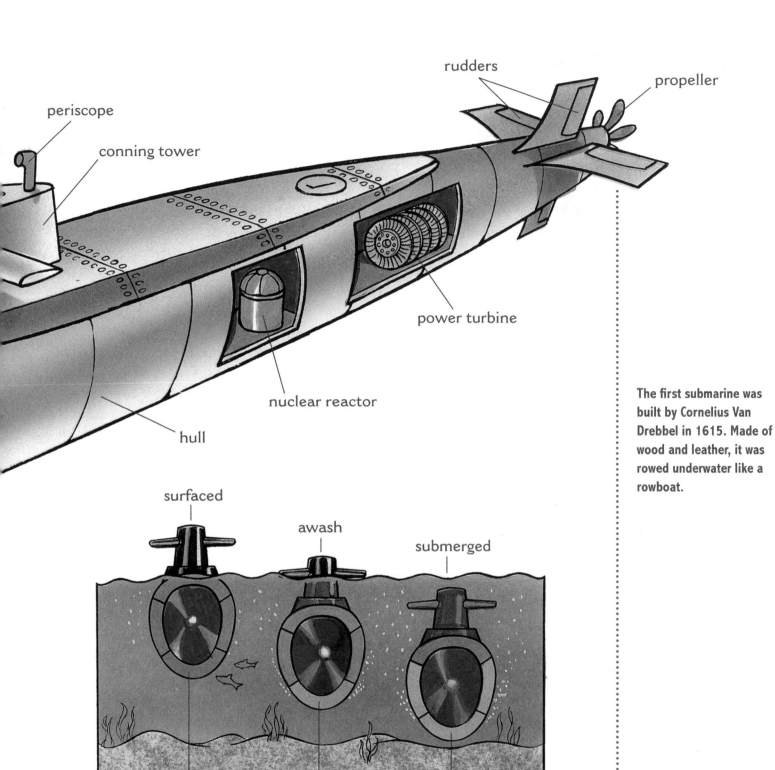

periscope

conning tower

rudders

propeller

power turbine

nuclear reactor

hull

surfaced

awash

submerged

empty ballast chamber

ballast chamber half full of water

full ballast chamber

The first submarine was built by Cornelius Van Drebbel in 1615. Made of wood and leather, it was rowed underwater like a rowboat.

A nuclear submarine does not have to come up to the surface until it needs more fuel. The nuclear submarines of the United States Navy can stay underwater for months before refueling.

Kite

Kites fly because the wind is strong enough to lift them up and away. As the kite tilts into the wind, the air pressure on the front of the kite is greater than the air pressure on its back. This creates the force called *lift*. Because of lift, the kite moves upward.

Kites come in many shapes and sizes, from the flat, diamond-shaped kite to the fancy Chinese dragon kite. The diamond-shaped kite is made of paper or light fabric that is stretched over two crossed sticks. The crossed sticks make a frame. The stick that runs the length of the kite is the longer of the two. The place where the two sticks cross is the *point of balance*.

A string runs through the edge of the paper and shows through at the four corners of the diamond. The string at the corners fits into notches in the ends of the crossed sticks.

Another string is tied to each end of the longer stick. This string is loose and longer than the stick. It is called a *bridle cord*. It is tied to the *flying line*, a long string that wraps around the *winder*. It is easier to hold the winder than to hold a single string. The winder keeps the flying line from tangling.

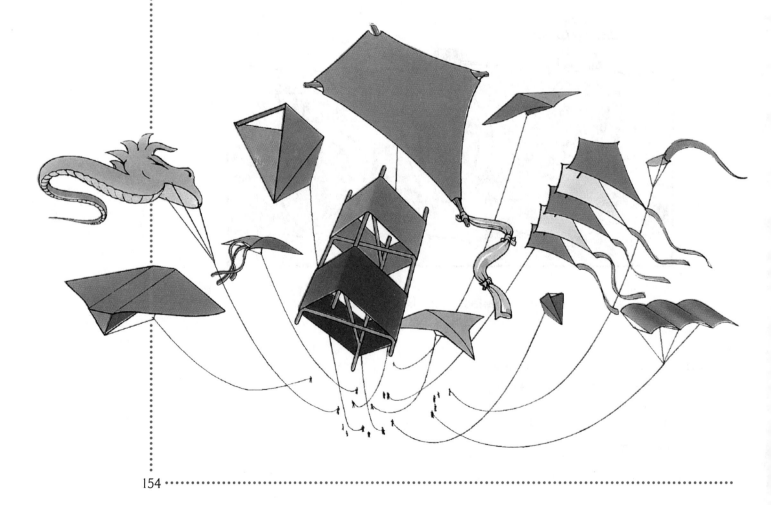

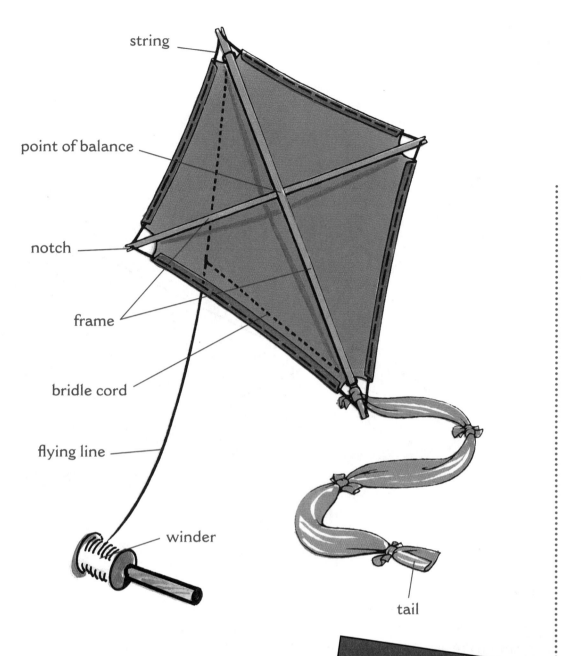

string

point of balance

notch

frame

bridle cord

flying line

winder

tail

A *tail* is fixed to the bottom of the kite. The tail helps balance the kite as it flies. It keeps the bottom end of the kite pointing down, so the kite flies at the right angle to the wind.

It is best to run down a treeless hill to put your kite in the air. When you feel a breeze, let out a few yards of string from your winder. Stand with your back to the breeze and watch your kite. You can feel it tugging and needing more string. Let out as much as you can without letting the kite swoop down. If it begins to drop, rewind some of the string. Once your kite is high in the sky, it will stay there.

Kites have not always been toys. In China, as far back as 1000 B.C., they were used for religious purposes, fishing, military signaling, and spying on the enemy in battle. During a battle, a man lay spread-eagled on the upper surface of a huge kite as he watched the movements of the enemy. In Europe in the 1500s, the kite became a plaything for children and got its name. It is named after the kite, a bird of the hawk family.

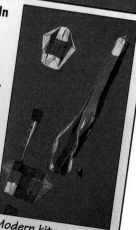

Modern kites come in all shapes and sizes.

Glider

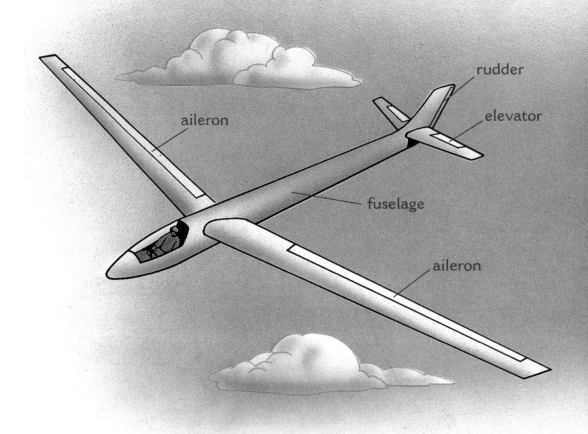

rudder

aileron

elevator

fuselage

aileron

In 1930, five men aboard a glider ran into a hailstorm. The glider was taking on a thick coating of ice. The men checked their parachutes and jumped. As they fell, a powerful wind suddenly lifted the men to the top of a cloud. There, they were coated with ice. Then they began to fall again, only to be carried up by another wind. Over and over, the same thing happened. Soon the men were covered with ice. They had been turned into human hailstones. With their parachutes open, the men finally drifted to earth. Amazingly, they were injured but not killed.

A glider is a plane that doesn't have an engine or carry fuel. It flies by riding on the air currents that flow over the planet.

A glider is shaped like a regular plane, but it is built to stay in the air without power. It has a longer wingspan for extra lift. The main body, called the *fuselage,* is sleek and thin so it won't drag against the air as it flies. Like an airplane, the glider has *ailerons, elevators,* and a *rudder* to help control how it moves. The elevators let the pilot make the glider go up or down. The ailerons and rudder make it turn. A glider can't be too heavy, so most only hold the pilot and one passenger.

To take off, you need to get your glider moving fast. Usually, the glider is towed behind a powered airplane. Then, you can make your glider rise by riding on the wind that blows upward on a hill. You can also move upward on a *thermal,* an air current that rises up from Earth's surface.

Thermals are made of warm air, and since warm air rises, thermals push gliders up, too. Warm air rises because it is lighter than cold air.

To find thermals, you look for natural signs. Thermals are found over warm areas of land and under clouds. You might look for certain cloud patterns, or you might see birds soaring on the currents without flapping their wings. Once you find one, you can soar, enjoying the quiet, gentle ride of a glider!

Toy Airplane

A toy airplane works almost like a real airplane. Both have wings, tail fins, and at least one engine.

Toy planes are made of a very light wood called balsa. After the wings have been cut from the balsa, they are bent to curve down at the edges. This wing shape causes *lift* when air passes over and under it. The air moving over the top of the wing must go farther—and faster—to catch up with the air passing under the bottom. This makes the air pressure under the wings greater than the air pressure on top. This difference in pressure "lifts" the wing.

The wings are really made of one piece of wood. The wood piece fits through a slot in the plane's body. The wings are the same length. Slots near the plane's tail hold the *fins*. The fins keep the plane flying straight.

The propeller at the nose of the plane hooks to a rubber band. The other end of the rubber band is fixed to the plane farther down the plane's body. When the propeller is spun around, the rubber band winds up. The winding rubber band stores energy—just as when a real plane's tank is filled with fuel. Letting go of the propeller makes the rubber band unwind. The unwinding rubber band supplies the energy for the plane to fly.

Because the rubber band is hooked to the propeller, the propeller spins as the rubber band unwinds. The spinning propeller pushes air backward. This makes the plane go forward.

Toy airplanes are used by the United States military. Some models carry small cameras. These send back either photos or videotape of what the enemy is doing. They can be guided to their targets by computerized remote-control devices. Other models carry small bombs.

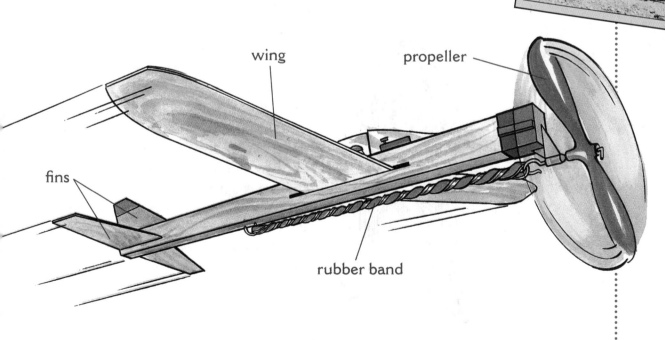

wing

propeller

fins

rubber band

Fireworks

Gunpowder makes fireworks explode. Gunpowder is a black powder mixture of chemicals and charcoal. This mixture burns and explodes.

The colors of fireworks come from metals. Metals burn different colors. For example, iron burns the color of gold; barium burns green. The metals are made into a powder. The powdered metals are then made into pellets. Pellets look like small bullets. The pellets in a firework are called stars. The stars are packed in the shell (or tube) of the firework.

The shells are loaded by professionals into launching tubes. The *fuse* is lit. The fuse is a kind of string that burns. Fireworks have long fuses so that the person who lights them has time to

move away. Some fireworks have electric starters so a person can start them from a safe distance.

A *rocket* is one kind of firework. Its shell has four levels of stars and gunpowder. A quick-burning fuse lights both ends of the rocket at the same time. The bottom layer—the layer of gunpowder—is lit first. It explodes and sends the shell into the sky.

A *time-delay fuse* explodes the other three levels one at a time. As each level explodes, it creates colors. The top level explodes high in the sky. This level might be made of more gunpowder and red stars. A few seconds later, the next level is lit. This level might have blue stars. Another time-delay fuse lights the *flash*

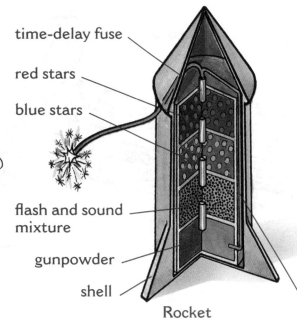

time-delay fuse

red stars

blue stars

flash and sound mixture

gunpowder

shell

Rocket

quick-burning fuse

Sparkler

and sound mixture. The flash and sound mixture is made of aluminum. It is the aluminum that makes the bright white light and loud noise.

Sparklers are another kind of firework. A sparkler is made by dipping a wire into a soup of gunpowder and a *binder*. The binder holds the gunpowder on the wire. Mixed into the soup might be one of the powdered metals that burn in color. The mixture dries and hardens on the wire. Then the wire is dipped in aluminum. The gunpowder mixture burns, the aluminum makes sparks, and the metals make colors.

Fireworks can be dangerous. A shell could explode too early or fall back to the ground to explode. A sparkler could start a fire on the grass if it is not burned out. In the United States people who shoot fireworks must have permission to do so. They are often firefighters. They wear protective clothing and goggles when they set off fireworks. A fire truck and ambulance stand by in case of danger.

Helicopter

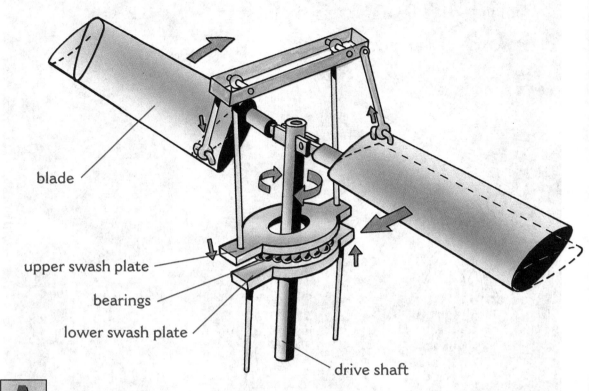

blade

upper swash plate

bearings

lower swash plate

drive shaft

A helicopter can take off straight up, fly backward, and hold still in the air. These abilities make a helicopter different from an airplane, which can only move up when it is moving forward.

A helicopter doesn't have wings, but it does have rotors. Rotors do the same job for a helicopter as wings do for a plane. A rotor is made of a *drive shaft*—an upright, turning post—and *blades* that attach to the drive shaft. The blades have the same special shape as airplane wings. Like airplane wings, they

create a force called *lift* as they move through the air. (See pages 162-163.) Lift makes the blades move up, taking the rest of the helicopter along with them.

If the helicopter had only one rotor spinning all by itself, the body of the helicopter would start spinning in the opposite direction when it lifted off the ground. The *tail rotor* solves this problem. It blows air to one side, which balances the spinning motion of the top rotor.

To steer the helicopter, the blade on one side must be tilted at a different angle from the blade on the other side. The steeper blade will have more lift, so the helicopter will rise more on that side. Then, the helicopter will move in that direction.

Tilting the blades is done with a pair of metal plates, called *swash plates*. The upper swash plate turns with the blades, while the lower swash plate stays still.

The first helicopter was made of bamboo! By using six propellers, its inventors were able to get it to rise ten feet in the air. But because there was no way of controlling it, the helicopter had to be steadied by ropes anchored to the ground. In 1907, a Frenchman named Cornu built the first helicopter that could fly without ropes to hold it steady. The machine rose 6 feet in the air and stayed off the ground for 21 seconds. As far back as the 1400s, though, Leonardo da Vinci had thought of a flying machine that looked a lot like a helicopter. He drew pictures of the machine in his journals.

Paul Cornu with his helicopter

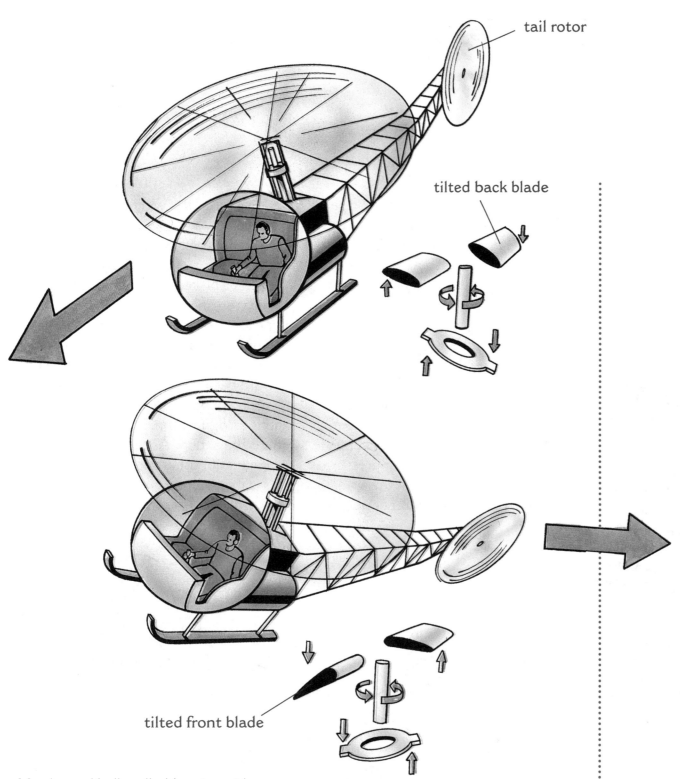

tail rotor

tilted back blade

tilted front blade

Hard metal balls called *bearings* ride between the plates so they move smoothly against each other.

When the upper swash plate moves up on one side, it makes whichever blade is swinging by on that side tilt at an angle. The blade returns to normal as it spins around to the other side. In forward flight, the blade in back tilts more. In backward flight, the front blade is tilted more.

To *hover,* or hold still in the air, both blades are tilted at the same angle, so the helicopter doesn't move forward or backward. The blades create just enough lift to balance out the weight of the helicopter.

Airplane

The wing of an airplane—the part that keeps it in flight—is like a bird's wing. Both are curved on top and almost flat on the bottom. This shape is an *airfoil*. When the airplane moves forward, air flows over the top and bottom of the airfoil. Since the top of the airfoil is curved, the air that flows over it has farther to go than the air that flows under it. The air moving over the top of the airfoil must go faster to catch up with the air passing under the bottom. The faster the air moves, the lower its pressure is. This makes the air pressure under the wing greater than the air pressure on top. This difference in pressure "lifts" the wing—it pushes the airfoil up.

To create the flow of air, the plane must move forward. To move forward, most small planes use one or more *propeller* engines. The engine of a propeller plane is like the engine of a car. The propeller is like the blades of a fan. The propeller engines make the plane fly forward because every *action* has an equal and opposite *reaction*. As the blades turn, they throw air backward. This is the action. As the air flows backward, it pushes the plane forward. This is the reaction.

Many others tried to build airplanes before Orville and Wilbur Wright. One try was "The Bird-Powered Flying Machine." The inventor attached several large birds to a balloon. The idea was that they would flap their wings and the balloon would fly away. The birds refused to flap their wings, though, and the flying machine stayed on the ground.

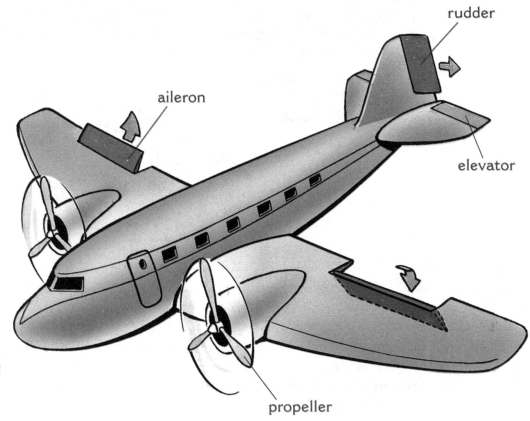

rudder

aileron

elevator

propeller

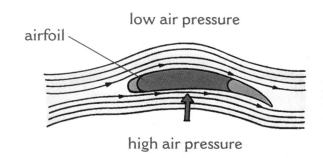

low air pressure

airfoil

high air pressure

In today's small planes, the pilot steers the plane with two pedals and a control column. Moving the control column drives the *elevators.* The elevators are the fins that run across the tail. Pulling back on the control column tips the elevators up. Tipping the elevators up creates a stream of air that pushes the *tail* down. The *nose* of the plane points up, and the plane climbs. Turning the elevators down creates a stream of air that pushes the tail up. The nose of the plane points down, and the plane drops.

The control column also moves the *ailerons.* The ailerons are the flaps on the edges of the wings. The ailerons move up and down to change the shape of the wings. The pilot uses the ailerons to roll the plane right or left.

The pedals move the *rudder.* The rudder is a movable fin on the plane's tail. When the rudder points straight back, air flows right past it. The plane flies straight ahead. When the rudder moves to one side, the air pushes against that side, sending the plane in a new direction. A pilot uses the rudder along with the ailerons to bank the plane in a smooth turn.

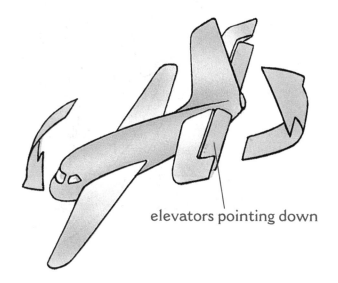

nose

tail

elevators pointing up

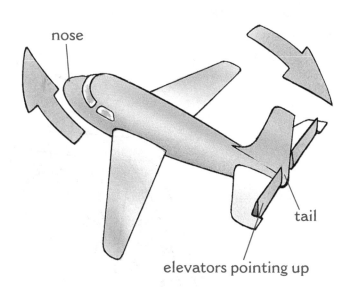

elevators pointing down

The first flight attendants had to be registered nurses. Passenger planes in the early days were unheated and unpressurized, so the airlines wanted nurses on hand to tend to the comfort and health of the passengers. The flight attendants had duties on the ground, too. They carried passengers' baggage, cleaned the interior of the airplane, helped the pilot and mechanics push the machine in and out of hangars, and helped refuel the plane.

The first flight attendants' uniforms even looked like nurses' uniforms.

Jet Engine

There are different types of jet engines, including ramjets, turbojets, and turbofan engines. Jet engines have power because every action has an equal and opposite reaction. The *action* is a stream of burning gases bursting out of the back of the engine. The *reaction* is the plane moving forward.

1. Here we'll look at how a *turbofan* jet engine works. To start the action, a large fan pulls air through the engine's *front intake*.

2. The air goes into the *compressor*. The compressor is a core surrounded by fanlike blades.

Airplanes powered by jet engines travel at 450 to 600 miles per hour. The fastest jets can reach "Mach 3." Flying at Mach 3 is flying at three times the speed of sound. That's nearly 2,000 miles per hour!

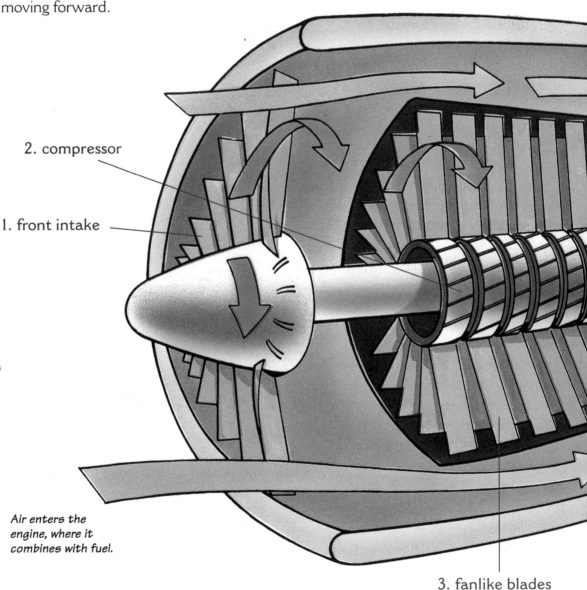

2. compressor

1. front intake

Air enters the engine, where it combines with fuel.

3. fanlike blades

3. The air flows through the sets of fanlike blades that *compress,* or squeeze, it. Air heats up as it is compressed.

4. The hot air goes into a *combustion chamber.* Fuel comes into the combustion chamber through nozzles. The hot compressed air mixes with fuel deep in the combustion chamber. The fuel catches fire and burns.

5. The burning fuel gives off very hot gases. The hot gases shoot past the *turbine blades.* The movement of gases makes the turbine turn. As the turbine turns, it turns the compressor. The compressor blades compress more air, and the action goes on and on.

6. The gases shoot out the back of the engine. This action causes an equal and opposite reaction. The plane is pushed forward.

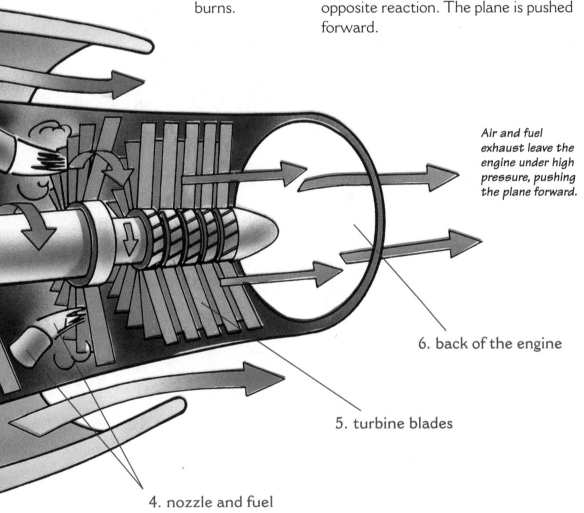

Air and fuel exhaust leave the engine under high pressure, pushing the plane forward.

6. back of the engine

5. turbine blades

4. nozzle and fuel

Centuries ago, in ancient China, a man named Wan-hu tried to invent a device based on ideas similar to those behind the jet engine. Around 1000 B.C., he built a flying machine made of two kites attached to a chair. He tied 42 rockets to the chair. Wan-hu seated himself in the chair, and all 42 rockets were lit at the same time. Unfortunately, the paper kites, the wooden chair, and the inventor all blew up in one huge bang.

Parachute

pilot chute

air vent

canopy

main chute

lines

harness

packed emergency chute

During World War I, the Germans invented the "observer gun." It shot a man into the air. A parachute opened, and the man floated to the ground while looking through binoculars at what the enemy was doing. Usually they were shooting at him!

An object falling toward Earth falls very fast unless its *surface area* is made bigger. Surface area is the size of something when it is laid out flat. When its surface area is made bigger, the falling object slows down. *Friction*—the rubbing between the air and the object—slows the falling object. A parachute has enough surface area to slow a falling person so he or she can land safely on the ground.

Before leaving the plane, the parachutist folds the chute, fits it into a pack, and carries it on his or her back. Parachutists carry an emergency chute, too. The parachutist wears a *harness*. The harness is made up of straps that go around the body, between the legs, and over the shoulders. The chute's *lines* are attached to the shoulder straps.

After jumping from the plane, the parachutist waits a few seconds before pulling the *rip cord*. The rip cord is attached to a pin. When the pin is pulled out, the *pilot chute* pops out. When air catches the pilot chute, it pulls the main parachute out of the pack.

Once air fills the main chute, the parachutist's fall slows from at most 176 feet per second to only a few feet per second. A parachute ride could be rocky if there were no *vents* in the *canopy*. (A vent is an air hole.) The vent at the very top lets air flow out of the canopy evenly. Because the vent is in the center, air flows through the chute in a straight line. Without the top vent, air would spill out from the sides of the chute. The parachutist would swing dizzily all the way down.

Rocket Engine

A basic rocket engine has tanks filled with fuel. When the fuel is lit, it burns, releasing hot gases. The rocket moves because every action has an equal and opposite reaction. The *action* is the hot gases exploding out of the rocket. The hot gases come out with great force. This action causes a *reaction*. The reaction is the forward motion (blasting off) of the rocket. The reaction has the equal force in the opposite direction. Because the gases shoot down, the rocket shoots up.

There are several types of rockets, including solid-fuel rockets and liquid-fuel rockets. Fireworks on the Fourth of July are launched into the sky by solid-fuel rockets. Solid-fuel rockets have tubes packed with fuel. The fuel is in solid form.

The *Saturn 5* used on the moon missions is a liquid-fuel rocket. Liquid-fuel rockets have separate tanks. One tank carries the liquid fuel—usually hydrogen. Another tank carries liquid oxygen. Fuel cannot burn without oxygen. Space rockets burn so much fuel so fast, they need more oxygen than the air around them can give. Also, there is no oxygen in outer space. The rockets must carry their own oxygen.

The fuel and oxygen are combined in the *combustion chamber.* Pumps push the fuel and oxygen into the chamber. *Valves* start and stop the flow of fuel and oxygen. Once in the combustion chamber, the fuel and oxygen burn and explode. The burning gases shoot out through the bottom of the rocket.

fuel tank

oxygen tank

pumps

valves

combustion chamber

burning gases

Scientists estimate there are approximately 7,000 pieces of "space junk" in orbit around Earth. Most space junk is pieces of rockets and fuel tanks that were pushed off during launch.

Space Shuttle

When it blasts into orbit, a space shuttle uses five rocket engines. Three rocket engines run on liquid fuel. The other two run on solid fuel. As the shuttle moves toward its orbit, it lets the two solid-fuel rocket *boosters* fall. The boosters are rocket engines that give the shuttle the extra power it needs to lift off. Once the shuttle reaches its orbit, it lets go of the very large fuel tank it carried for its liquid-fuel rockets. The liquid-fuel rockets and their smaller fuel tanks stay on the shuttle.

Rockets in the tail of the shuttle steer the ship into orbit. Other rockets in the nose and the tail make the ship stay on its path for the whole trip.

Each shuttle carries a different *payload*. A payload is the group of things that are to be carried into space. Some payloads are top secret. Most have been *satellites*. A satellite is an object that orbits another object, such as Earth. The Moon is a natural Earth satellite. Artificial satellites have been built to gather information—such as pictures—about our world.

The payload rides in a large *cargo bay* area. The bay opens and a long *robot arm* lifts the load up and out. The arm also pulls loads—such as satellites that need repairs—into the bay. A crew member works the robot arm from a control panel inside the shuttle. An astronaut works in the cargo area. A *tether line* keeps the astronaut from floating into space.

The shuttle cabin has two sections. The upper section is the flight deck. This is where the mission commander and the pilot ride. The lower section is where the crew sleeps and works. It also has a

The space shuttle launched on April 6, 1984, carried more than 3,000 honeybees. Scientists wanted to know if the honeycombs bees built in space were the same as the honeycombs they built on Earth. Although the honeycombs were different at first, the bees soon were building honeycombs that were no different from those made on Earth.

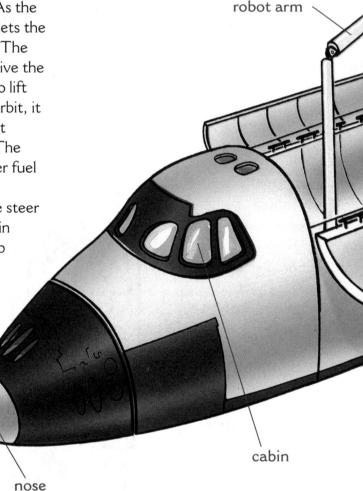

robot arm

cabin

nose

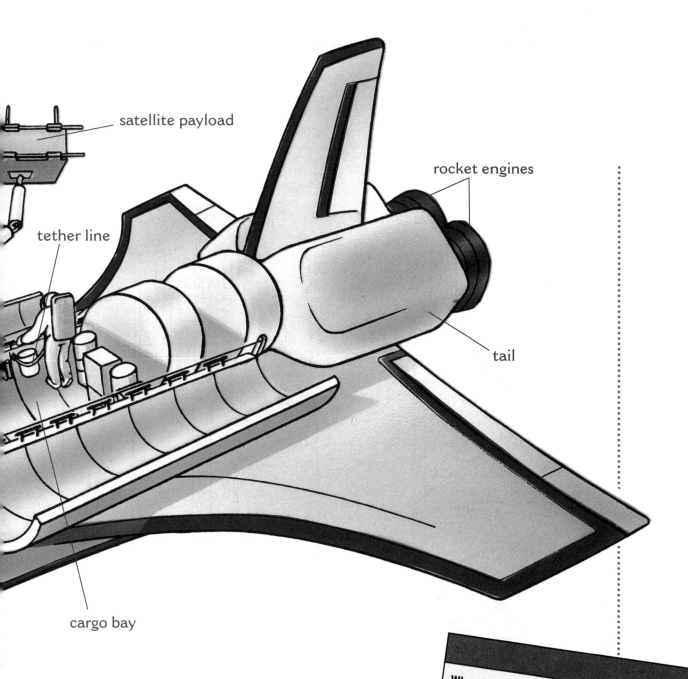

satellite payload

tether line

rocket engines

tail

cargo bay

kitchen where the crew members prepare their food. The shuttle can carry seven astronauts.

The air pressure inside the cabin is like the air pressure on Earth. The astronauts don't have to wear space suits while working, eating, and sleeping in the cabin. They only have to wear space suits when they go outside the shuttle.

Rockets in the nose and tail of the shuttle steer the ship out of its orbit when the mission is over. The shuttle comes back to Earth at a speed of almost 16,000 miles per hour. It slows to about 200 miles per hour before gliding to a stop.

When it reached outer space, the space shuttle used to fly with both its cargo bay doors completely open. Opening the doors helped heat to escape. However, the shuttle now has to fly with one door partly closed. This is done to protect fragile cooling loops on the interior of the doors from being hit by pieces of orbiting "space junk."

Shuttle Launch Vehicle

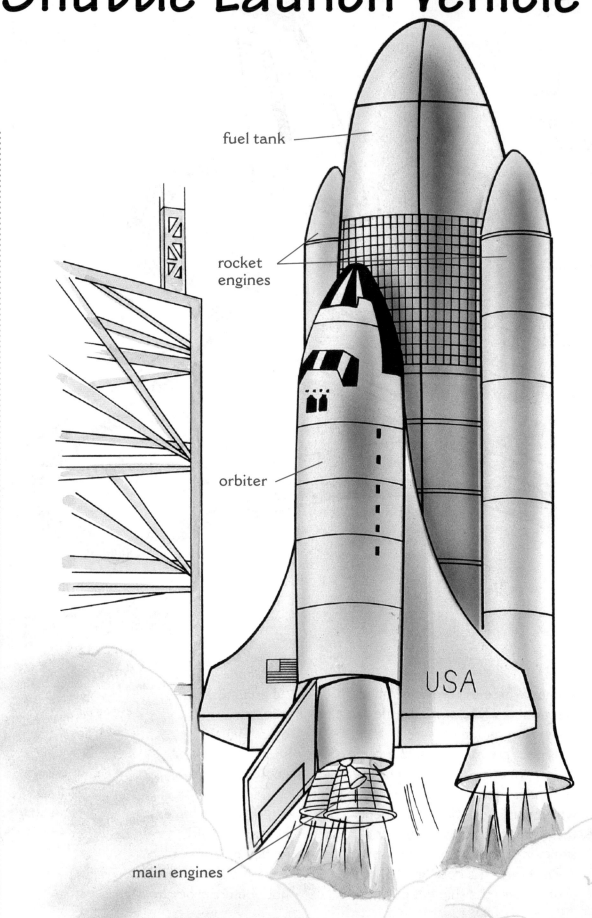

fuel tank

rocket engines

orbiter

main engines

Before space travel became a reality, scientists realized what their biggest obstacle was. It was breaking free of Earth's gravity. Many ideas were suggested. One of the first was using hot-air balloons to tow a "space glider" into outer space. Another was using a giant metal slingshot to launch the craft. Recently, scientists have experimented with a space cannon that would shoot very small objects into space. The objects launched by the cannon do not have engines.

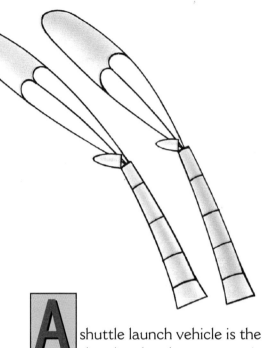

A shuttle launch vehicle is the shuttle, plus the extra engines and fuel that give the shuttle power for the lift into space. The launch vehicle is made up of four parts. The parts are the *orbiter* (the shuttle), two *rocket engines,* and a large *fuel tank.*

One rocket engine is attached to each side of the large fuel tank. These rocket engines are *solid-fuel* engines. They are filled with fuel in a solid form.

The large fuel tank is made up of two tanks. One tank holds liquid *hydrogen.* Hydrogen is the fuel. The other tank holds liquid *oxygen.* The hydrogen fuel needs oxygen to burn. There is not enough oxygen in our *atmosphere* (the layer of air that surrounds Earth) for the fuel to burn fast enough to keep the shuttle going. And there is no oxygen in

space. That's why the launcher carries its own supply of oxygen. Together, hydrogen and liquid oxygen give energy to the orbiter's three main engines.

Just before the launch countdown reaches zero, the fuel and the oxygen from the large tank are pumped into the orbiter's three main engines. Four seconds later, the two solid-fuel rockets are lit. With all five engines roaring, the shuttle lifts off into space!

The two solid-fuel rockets burn out in a few minutes. As they burn out, they are pushed off and away from the large tank. Parachutes on each rocket open, and the rockets float gently back to Earth. They can be refilled and used again.

After eight minutes, the large fuel tank runs dry and leaves the shuttle. The tank breaks up and falls into the ocean. It cannot be used again.

Space Suit

Out in space there is no air for a human to breathe. The temperature can get hot or cold enough to kill a person. A space suit surrounds an astronaut with an *atmosphere* in which he or she can live. Atmosphere is the air that surrounds Earth.

The suit is made in several parts. The inner layer is the *liquid cooling and ventilation garment* (LCVG). A pump keeps a cooling liquid flowing through the LCVG. The LCVG keeps the astronaut at a comfortable, healthy temperature.

The outer shell of the suit is *airtight*. Air cannot leak out of it. It holds the air needed to keep the astronaut alive. Bottles attached to the back of the suit feed oxygen gas into the suit.

The outer shell is made in parts. The top part of the body has gloves. The pants have built-in-boots. A helmet covers the astronaut's head. A microphone and earphones are built into the helmet. These let the astronaut talk with the shuttle crew. To operate the radio, the astronaut uses controls on the chest of the suit.

To move around in space, an astronaut uses a *manned maneuvering unit*. It is like a rocket-pack fastened onto the back of the suit. It moves the astronaut through space.

In 1837 in London, a young woman answered the door. Standing there was a man wearing a tight-fitting garment that looked like a glossy white space suit. His head was completely enclosed by a glass globe. On the ends of his arms were sharp metallic claws. When the woman screamed, the man bounded away with 30-foot leaps. In the decades that followed, "The Jumping Man from Outer Space," as he was called, was seen by hundreds of people all over England. He was last seen in 1904, then disappeared.

Can you imagine how a person in the 1800s would feel if confronted by a person in a modern space suit?

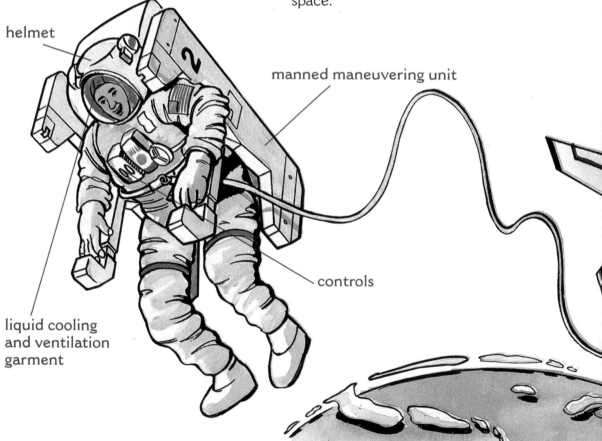

helmet

manned maneuvering unit

controls

liquid cooling and ventilation garment

Electricity

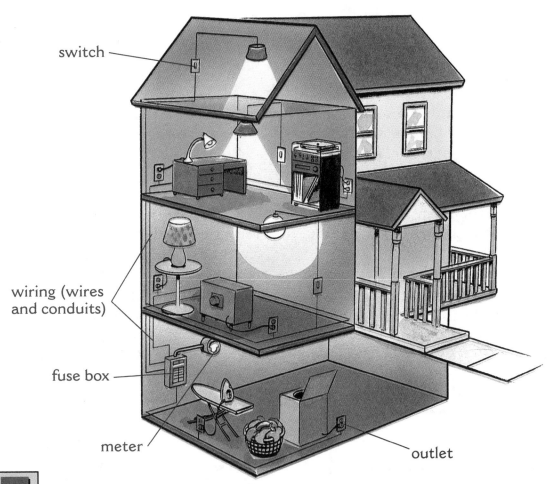

switch

wiring (wires and conduits)

fuse box

meter

outlet

Electricity runs through a *circuit*. A circuit is a loop. You make a circuit when you plug a lamp cord into a wall outlet and flip a switch. Flipping a wall switch stops and starts the electricity flowing through the circuit.

Electricity comes into your house through the *meter*. The meter keeps track of how much electricity you use, so the electric company can tell how much electricity you must pay for. From there, it passes through a *fuse box* (or circuit breaker box). Fuses and circuit breakers keep the wires from getting too hot. If the wires get too hot, they can be dangerous. If a wire becomes dangerous, the fuse or circuit breaker stops the flow of electricity. When the

problem is repaired, the electricity can go through the circuit again.

Electrical wires run through your house inside a thin pipe or through a special plastic material. When the house is built, an electrician installs wires that go to each outlet and switch in your house. The electricity runs through these wires.

Let's take the example of a lamp. As you push the plug into an outlet, you are adding a piece to the circuit. Electricity flows out of the outlet and through the cord. Flip the lamp switch on and electricity runs through a thin wire inside the lightbulb. This wire glows brightly when electricity heats it.

In 1985, a man by the name of Bill Borst invented a clock that runs on potato power! It gets its electricity from two potatoes. Each potato has a metal bolt stuck through it. One bolt is made of zinc, the other of copper. The metal reacts with acid in the potato to create an electric current, which runs along a wire into the clock.

POTATO POWER

Electricity

The electricity in your home comes from a power plant. Some power plants get their power from water.

1. The water flow of a river can be controlled by a dam. A dam has walls. Water flows through channels in the walls.

2. When the water rushes through the channels in the dam's walls, it creates pressure.

3. Water pressure turns the blades on the shaft of the *generator*. The generator transforms the energy of the flowing water into electricity.

4. As the shaft turns, it makes electricity, using the principles of magnets and magnetic fields.

5. Electricity flows out of the generator and through *power lines*. The lines lead to a *transformer* near your house.

6. The transformer brings the power down to a level that is safe for use in your

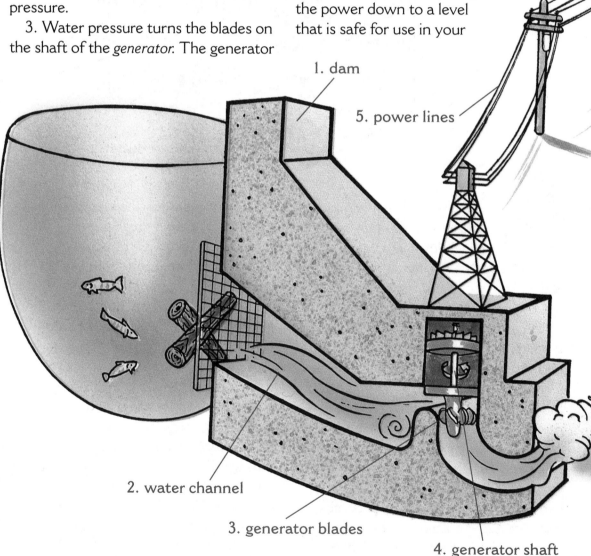

1. dam

5. power lines

2. water channel

3. generator blades

4. generator shaft

6. transformer

home. Transformers can be
seen on top of power-line poles.
The power lines are strung between the
poles. Electricity travels through
another line to your house.
Many homes and factories
receive their electricity through
underground wires.
Electricity flows through wiring that is
between the walls of your house. The
wires run in pairs. The wires run to all
the outlets and switches. The outlets let
you plug into the electrical power that
runs through the wiring. Switches stop
and start the flow of the electricity.

Solar Energy

The sun gives off energy in the form of sunlight. It is solar energy. This energy can be collected and used. It can heat homes, make electricity, and even power cars! Sunlight can be collected all year round.

Using solar energy means using the sun's rays. The sun's rays can be collected with a *passive solar collector*. This kind of collector is used to heat homes. It is called "passive" because it has no moving parts. It is made of a special glass. Sunlight comes in on one side, passes through, and heats the room on the other side. Very little heat leaves through the glass when the sun is not shining.

An *active solar collector* uses moving parts to collect the sun's energy. The moving parts are motors, fans, and pumps. This kind of collector is used to heat water for washing and bathing. Copper *collector panels* are placed on the roof of the house. Copper tubes filled with liquid run through the collectors. As the liquid travels through the tubing, it gets hot. The hot liquid goes to a heat exchanger. The *heat exchanger* warms a

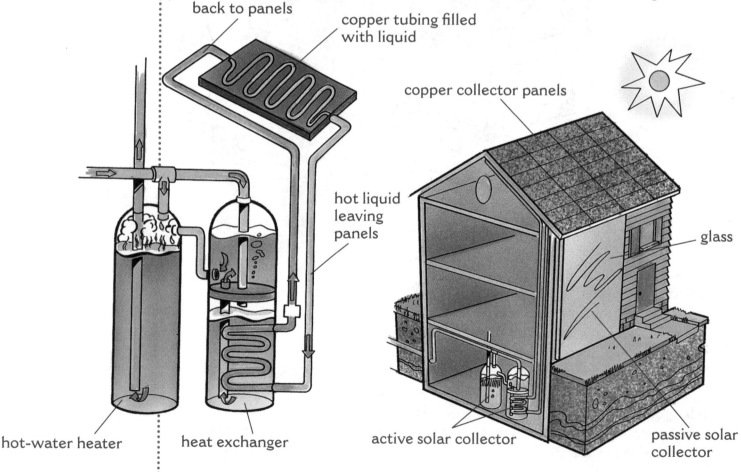

cooled liquid going back to panels

copper tubing filled with liquid

copper collector panels

hot liquid leaving panels

glass

hot-water heater

heat exchanger

active solar collector

passive solar collector

collector panels

tank of water. The warmed water is pumped into a hot-water heater. It is stored there. The water may now be heated even more. Then it can be used for washing and bathing.

Once the liquid in the tubing goes to the heat exchanger, it loses its heat to the water. This cooled liquid is pumped back to the collector panels for reheating. The liquid does not freeze while running through the panels in the winter.

Another type of solar collector changes sunlight into electricity. The best example of this kind of collector is found in a solar-powered calculator.

Some people are experimenting with the idea of a solar-powered car. Cars that run on solar energy would use these solar collector panels to collect energy. A battery-powered motor would run the car. The battery would get its energy from the collector panels on the car. The car could run on the battery's stored energy even when the sun is not shining.

The idea may have started 4,000 years ago in ancient Egypt. It is thought that the pyramids were built in such a way that they could be lighted inside without the use of smoky torches and lamps. Instead, polished bronze shields may have been set up to reflect sunlight down into the deepest rooms. Today, solar scientists are working on the same idea for lighting buildings. They have invented heliostats, solar mirrors that direct light down a shaft on top of a building. Other mirrors then pick up the sunlight to light up inside rooms.

Nuclear Reactor

A nuclear reactor is a type of power plant. It produces electricity people can use to heat homes, run machines, and turn on lights. To do this, it uses an atomic fuel such as *uranium*.

Like all kinds of matter, uranium is made of *atoms*, tiny particles that are too small to see. In the nuclear reactor, atoms of uranium are split apart. This process, called a *nuclear reaction*, makes new, smaller atoms. It also gives off a huge amount of energy.

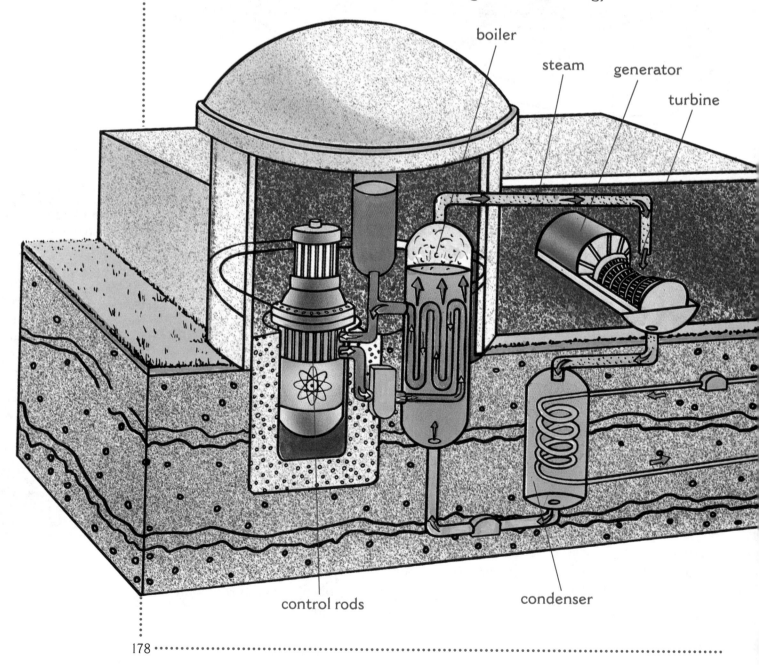

boiler

steam   generator

turbine

control rods

condenser

The *nucleus*—the center part of every atom—is made up of smaller parts called *neutrons* and *protons*. Inside the *reactor core*, neutrons are fired at uranium fuel rods. When a neutron hits a uranium nucleus, the nucleus breaks apart into two smaller nuclei (more than one nucleus are called "nuclei"). Energy is given off. Neutrons from the uranium nucleus also fly off, and they run into other nuclei. Those nuclei break apart, releasing more neutrons, and the reactions keep going. To slow down or stop the nuclear reactions, *control rods* are lowered into the reactor core. They pick up some of the neutrons before they can hit the fuel rods.

The first experimental nuclear reactor was a pretty strange affair. In December 1942, graphite blocks and uranium fuel were piled up in a handball court at the University of Chicago. Two men stood by with buckets of a chemical solution to be tossed onto the pile in case of a chain reaction. Then scientists slowly pulled out cadmium control rods they had placed in the pile. To their excitement, they discovered the rods were radioactive. Fourteen years after this first simple test, the first atomic power plant started operating.

The first nuclear power plant, Calder Hall in England.

Water runs through pipes around the reactor core. The water heats up as it picks up energy from the core. This helps cool the core and control the temperature of the reactions. If the temperature gets too high, parts of the nuclear reactor could melt down.

Next, the hot water travels through pipes inside the *boiler*. It heats up the water in the boiler until it turns to steam. The force of the steam turns a machine with fanlike blades, called a *turbine*, which turns a *generator*, which produces electricity. This electricity is sent out over power lines so it can be used in factories, offices, and homes.

The steam goes through a *condenser*, where it turns back into liquid water. Then, the water travels back to the boiler, and the cycle starts over again.

Lights and Switches

Fluorescent tube

plugs

mercury vapor

phosphor coating

Halogen light

filament

gas

quartz tube

supports for filament

Electricity was first used in the White House in 1891. Benjamin Harrison was the president of the United States then. Afraid of the lights, he would not touch the switches. Many times, he slept with the lights on.

Ametal glows when it is heated. It glows red first, then yellow, and finally white. The glow is *incandescence*.

An incandescent lightbulb has a thin metal wire strung in the middle of the bulb. The wire is a *filament*. Electricity flows through the metal filament. The heated filament glows white.

Most lamps use *tungsten* filament lightbulbs. Tungsten is a kind of metal. A tungsten bulb is a glass globe sealed to a brass base. The brass base screws into a light socket. Inside the globe, a glass stem holds up a wire frame. The wire frame is two wires that hold up each end of the filament. The filament is made of

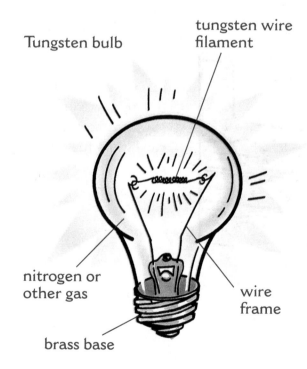

Tungsten bulb

tungsten wire filament

nitrogen or other gas

wire frame

brass base

a coil, or loop, of tungsten. Electricity flows through the wire and into the looped tungsten. The tungsten glows with a hot, white light. *Nitrogen,* a gas, fills the bulb. Sometimes other gases are used instead of nitrogen.

Streetlights and headlights use *halogen* light. The gas that fills the bulb has a chemical in it. The chemical makes the temperature hotter and the pressure higher in a halogen light than in a tungsten bulb. Because of this, the bulb is made of *quartz,* not glass. Quartz is a mineral that does not break as easily as glass.

The long tubes of light used in schools are *fluorescent* lights. A fluorescent tube has plugs at both ends. It does not have a filament. *Mercury vapor,* a gas, is inside the tube. Electricity flows through the gas from one end of the tube to the other. The gas gives off an invisible light when electricity flows through it. The light shines on a special coating on the inside of the tube called a *phosphor coating.* The coating glows brightly.

A light switch connects and disconnects wires. It does this by opening and closing *contacts* inside the switch. Contacts are made where two wires touch. Closing a contact lets electricity flow through. Opening a contact stops electricity from flowing through. Switching on a light connects the bulb to the electricity.

Switches open and close their contacts quickly to prevent sparks. Most do this by using a spring that snaps from open to closed when you flip the *switch*

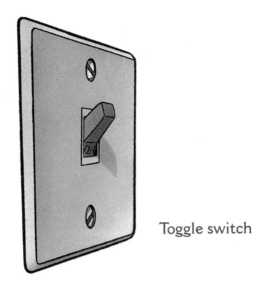

Toggle switch

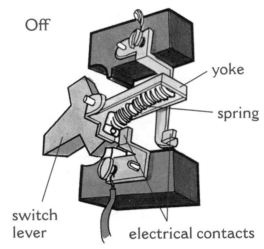

Off

yoke

spring

switch lever

electrical contacts

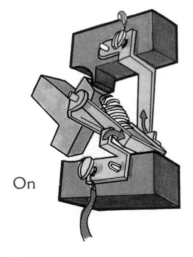

On

lever. Toggle switches use a spring. A *yoke* is the metal piece that connects the contacts. When the switch is in the "on" position, the yoke touches both contacts. Electricity flows to the light. Switched to "off," the yoke does not touch both contacts. Electricity does not flow to the light.

At first, it was considered "vulgar" and "lowly" to have electric lights in one's home. A "proper" home, it was believed, should be lit only by gas or candlelight.

Battery

A battery has metals and chemicals inside it that work together to produce electricity. The two main types of batteries are *dry cells* and *wet cells*. Flashlights and toys run on dry cells. Cars and trucks use wet cells.

Electricity is a flow of *electrons*. Electrons are tiny parts of *atoms*. Atoms are particles that are so tiny they are invisible to the eye. All things are made of atoms. A flow of electrons makes televisions, washing machines, and many other things work.

A battery has two *electrodes*. One electrode sends out electrons. Another electrode receives electrons.

The metal container that holds the parts of the dry cell battery is an electrode. It sends out electrons. Electricity flows out of this electrode. The center post, which is made of the chemical carbon, is another electrode. (The bump on the top of the battery is connected to the post.) The post receives the electrons. Electricity flows into this electrode. The space between the post and the outer container is filled with a paste. The paste is an *electrolyte*. The electrolyte makes the electricity flow from the container to the post. The flow of electricity between the electrodes is called a *circuit*. The circuit must be a complete circle for electricity to flow.

After a dry cell has been used for a long time, the electrolyte wears out. It cannot conduct electricity. The cell is "dead" and has to be replaced with a new one.

A wet cell battery works in much the same way. The difference is that it is made of thin metal sheets and a solution of acid. The sheets are made of lead and oxygen. The acid is the electrolyte. The electricity flows from some lead sheets through the acid to other lead sheets.

Most battery-operated machines, such as a radio, use more than one cell. The cells are loaded with the top of one cell touching the bottom of another. The flow of electricity is stronger than what one battery would produce alone.

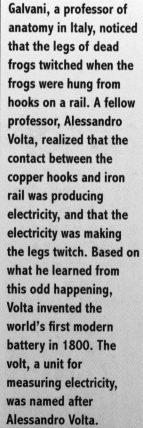

In the early 1780s, Luigi Galvani, a professor of anatomy in Italy, noticed that the legs of dead frogs twitched when the frogs were hung from hooks on a rail. A fellow professor, Alessandro Volta, realized that the contact between the copper hooks and iron rail was producing electricity, and that the electricity was making the legs twitch. Based on what he learned from this odd happening, Volta invented the world's first modern battery in 1800. The volt, a unit for measuring electricity, was named after Alessandro Volta.

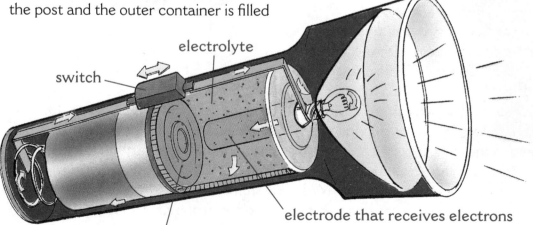

electrolyte

switch

electrode that receives electrons

electrode that sends out electrons

Weather Balloon

balloon

parachute

radiosonde

P|eople who predict the weather need to check conditions high up in the *atmosphere*, the layer of air that surrounds the planet. Weather balloons help them gather the information they need.

A weather balloon uses a gas-filled, rubber balloon. The gas inside the balloon is lighter than air, so the balloon floats upward. Hanging from the balloon is a package of instruments called a *radiosonde*.

Sensors in the radiosonde measure temperature, humidity (how much water is in the air), and air pressure (the weight of the air). The speed the balloon moves tells the speed of the wind in the upper atmosphere. A radio transmitter sends the information to weather stations on the ground.

As the balloon floats upward, the particles of air surrounding the balloon are more spread out. As a result, the air pressure is lower than it was near the ground. This change allows the gas in the balloon to *expand*, or take up more space, because the air outside the balloon isn't pushing on the balloon as hard. The rubber balloon stretches, getting bigger and bigger. A balloon that is five feet in diameter might expand until it is 20 feet across! Some balloons stretch until they pop. Then the radiosonde drifts back to Earth, hanging from a parachute.

Some other balloons start out only half-full of gas. They expand until they are full. These balloons can go higher in the atmosphere, up to 30 miles above the ground, and stay up for months.

The hot-air balloon was invented by Jacques and Joseph Montgolfier, two French brothers who ran a paper bag factory. They came up with the idea one day in 1782 when they filled a paper bag with hot air and found that it floated. In 1783, the brothers went for a test flight. When the Montgolfiers landed in a field, the local people thought they were being attacked by creatures from another planet. They proceeded to hack the balloon to pieces.

This engraving shows a balloon the Montgolfier brothers flew in 1784.

Weather Satellite

When the first astronauts orbited Earth and took photographs, scientists were excited by the pictures of clouds. They saw patterns in the way clouds move, and they realized these pictures could help them predict the weather. Since that time, many weather satellites have sent pictures back to Earth.

Weather satellites are simply cameras that orbit Earth, taking pictures of weather systems. They can track hurricanes and watch how air masses move. Photographs from weather satellites are used to make daily weather maps.

The *radiometer* is the satellite's camera. It can also sense and record heat from the ground. The satellite also contains *sounding units*. They measure temperature and moisture at different levels in the *atmosphere,* the layer of air that surrounds the planet. This information helps predict bad storms.

The satellite takes a picture and changes it into coded radio signals. Antennas send the radio signals back to stations on Earth. A computer on Earth translates the code and changes the signals back into a picture. You might have seen these kinds of pictures on a television weather report. A weather satellite also has *solar panels.* These change energy from sunlight into energy to power the satellite.

Some weather satellites orbit Earth from pole to pole. They circle the planet many times each day, taking about 1,000 pictures. These satellites are fairly close to Earth, so they can give "close-up" shots to tell us about local weather conditions.

Other satellites orbit around the equator, and they move at the same speed that the planet turns. As a result, each satellite rides along with Earth, hanging over its own spot on the ground. This type of satellite can show weather patterns over huge areas.

With all our advanced technology for understanding the weather, there still are some strange happenings we cannot explain. One day in 1958, Ms. R. Babington was at home when suddenly it began to rain. But when she looked up through the rain, she could see the sun shining. There wasn't a single cloud in the sky! When Ms. Babington walked out into the street, she realized the strangest thing of all. It was raining on her house, but nowhere else! Soon, people began to gather in the street. They could see that rain was falling from the sky, but there were no clouds! And the rain was falling in an area about 100 feet square. After more than two hours, the rain stopped. So far, no one has ever been able to explain this crazy, cloudless downpour.

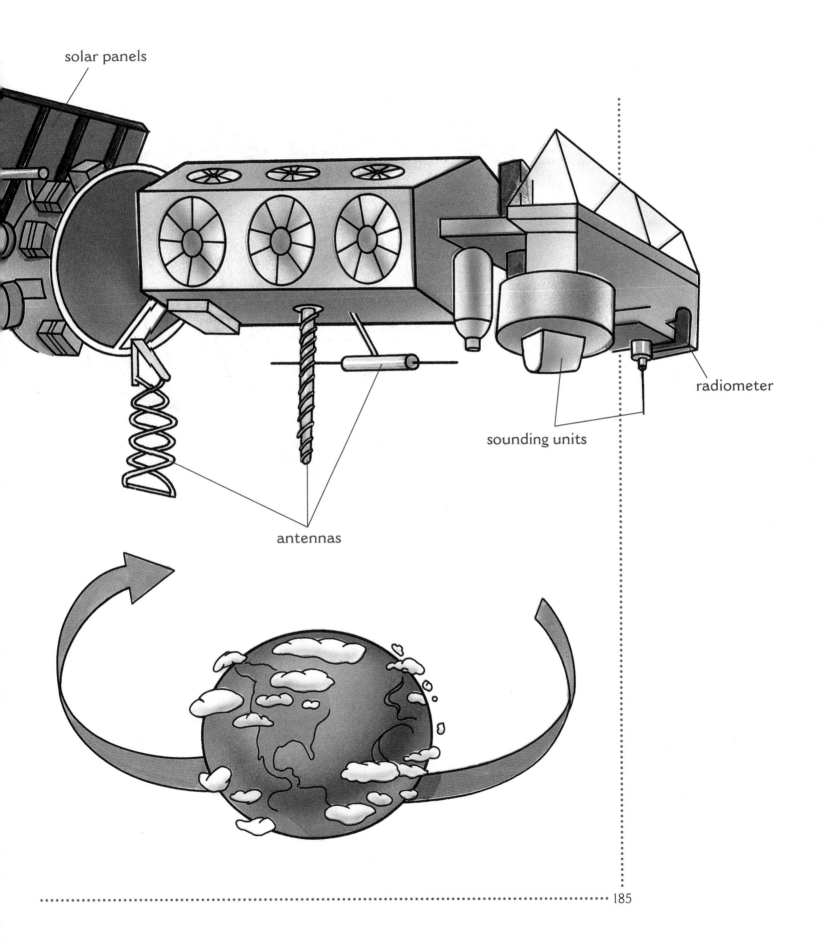

solar panels

radiometer

sounding units

antennas

Barometer

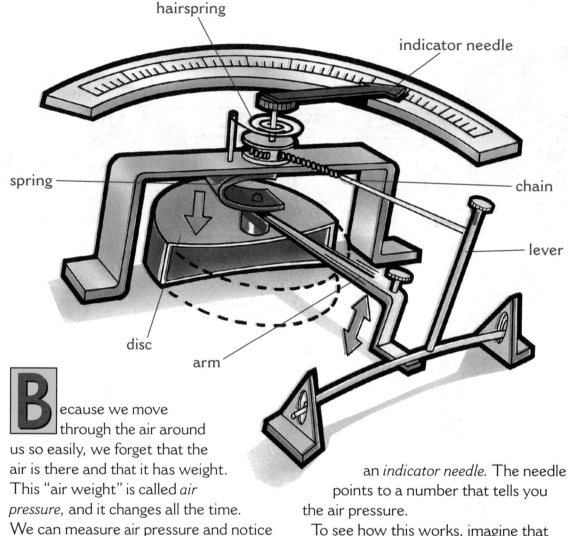

The barometer—and thermometer—went sky high one day in Portugal. On July 6, 1949, a freak heat wave hit the center of the country. The temperature rocketed up to 158 degrees! Not only is this the highest temperature ever recorded in Portugal, it is one of the highest recorded anywhere in the world. The temperature dropped after only two minutes. Many meteorologists have studied this strange, sudden heat wave. So far, they've been unable to come up with an explanation that makes sense.

B ecause we move through the air around us so easily, we forget that the air is there and that it has weight. This "air weight" is called *air pressure,* and it changes all the time. We can measure air pressure and notice its changes using a barometer.

You can use a barometer to tell how the weather will change. When the air pressure falls, you can expect cloudy, wet weather. A rise in air pressure means that you can expect drier conditions and sunny skies.

Inside a barometer is a closed, hollow *disc* that is almost empty of air. Air presses on the disc. The air squeezes the disc in if the air pressure is high. It lets the disc expand if the air pressure is low.

The rest of the barometer has parts that use the changes in the disc to move

an *indicator needle*. The needle points to a number that tells you the air pressure.

To see how this works, imagine that the air pressure is going up. When air pressure increases, the disc's top moves down. The movement of the disc moves a spring, an arm, and a lever, and the lever pulls on a chain. This action turns the post that holds the needle, making the needle move to the right. The needle shows that the air pressure has gone up. If the air pressure goes down, the disc moves up. The chain loosens, and a special kind of spring called a *hairspring* moves the needle back to the left. The reading on the barometer shows lower air pressure.

Thermometer

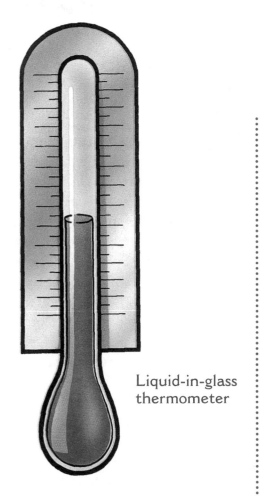

Liquid-in-glass thermometer

Y ou can tell when the temperature changes, but you need a thermometer to tell you exactly how much.

The most common kind of thermometer is called a *liquid-in-glass thermometer.* You may have used this type of thermometer to check how cold it is outside or to measure someone's body temperature. It has liquid inside a closed glass tube. If the liquid looks silver, it is *mercury,* a kind of metal. If it looks red, it is colored alcohol.

Either liquid will *expand,* or take up more space, when the temperature goes up. That makes the liquid move upward in the tube. When the temperature goes down, the liquid *contracts,* or shrinks, moving back down the tube. Since numbers are marked along the tube, you can tell how much the liquid has moved. The number tells you the temperature.

Another kind of thermometer, called a *bimetallic thermometer,* has a dial with a needle. Underneath the dial is a spring made of a ribbon of metal. The ribbon has two layers sandwiched together, usually brass and steel. Like liquids, the metal layers expand when they heat up and contract when they cool. But each layer expands and contracts a different amount. That difference makes the spring curl inward when it gets cold or open wider when it gets hot. You can tell how much the spring has moved by looking at a needle on the end of the spring. It points to a number on the dial, telling you the temperature. The *thermostat* that controls the heat in your home probably uses a bimetallic thermometer.

Bimetallic thermometer

Almost 400 years ago, a man named Santorio developed a device for measuring changes of body temperature during an illness. The idea was similar to today's thermometer. To operate the device, the patient held a glass bulb in his or her mouth. The bulb was connected by a glass tube to a container of colored water. As the patient's body temperature changed, the water level rose or fell.

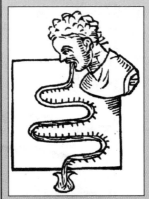

A drawing of Santorio's thermometer

Seismograph

The ground beneath our feet seems solid, but it moves all the time. Earth's surface is like a loose jigsaw puzzle, made of big pieces, called *plates*, that drift and bump into each other. Usually, the movements are so small we can't feel them. Sometimes one plate becomes wedged against another. The plates press very hard on each other. From time to time the plates break free and move very quickly. We feel those movements as earthquakes. When an earthquake occurs, it sends out waves of motion through the ground, like the waves when you drop a pebble into a pond. An instrument called a *seismograph* can detect these waves and tell us how much the ground has moved.

A seismograph is set firmly onto a solid rock surface beneath the soil. It has a spring that hangs down from a support. At the end of the spring is a bar with a weight and a pen on its end. When the ground moves in up-and-down waves, the spring bounces, which makes the pen move up and down.

The point of the pen runs along a drum that holds a paper tape. As the pen moves, it draws a line on the paper. The drum keeps turning, so the pen is always drawing on a clear space. If the pen draws high peaks on the paper, you know the waves that moved through the ground were also high. That tells you the earthquake was a powerful one.

Other kinds of seismographs use electronic parts instead of a pen and paper to record an earthquake's movements. They can be hooked up to a radio device to automatically send out earthquake reports.

When you hear about earthquakes in the United States, they usually happen on the West Coast. But did you know that the strongest quake recorded so far in the United States might have happened over 1,000 miles away in Missouri? Scientists think the New Madrid series of earthquakes in 1811-1812 might have reached 8.7 on the Richter scale. They are not sure because the seismograph was not yet invented at the time of the New Madrid quakes. They had to estimate the strength of the earthquakes based on the effects people observed afterward.

Reelfoot Lake was created by the great quakes. Land on one side of the Mississippi River dropped down several feet and river water flowed in to fill the space.

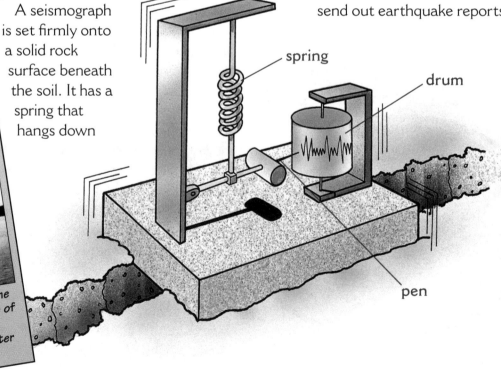

spring

drum

pen

Compass

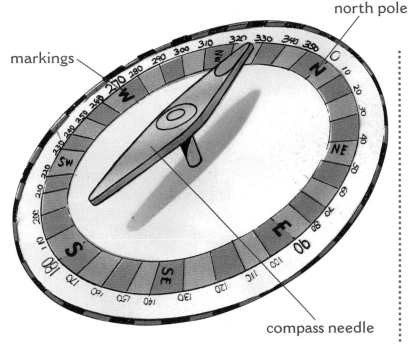

markings

north pole

compass needle

A compass needle always points north when the compass is held flat. When you face the direction the needle is pointing, you are facing north. South is behind you, east is to your right, and west is to your left.

Compasses work nearly everywhere on Earth. A compass is able to work because it is on Earth.

A *compass needle* is a magnet. A magnet is a metal that *attracts,* or pulls toward some other metals. *Magnetism* is an invisible force that flows through these metals. Magnetism makes metals attract each other.

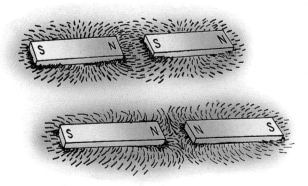

When the opposite poles of two magnets are placed near each other, the lines of force flow from one magnet to the other. The magnets attract each other.
When the like poles of two magnets are placed near each other, the lines of force flow back toward the other end of each magnet. The magnets repel each other.

A magnet has two ends. The ends are the *north pole* and the *south pole.* The magnetic force flows out of the north pole and around to the south pole. It then flows back into the south pole, through the magnet, back to the north pole. The area that the magnetic force flows through is the *magnetic field.*

Poles that are opposite poles attract each other. North poles attract south poles; south poles attract north poles. Poles that are like poles *repel* each other, or push each other away.

The planet Earth is a magnet. Earth has a north pole and a south pole. The compass needle lines up with Earth's lines of magnetic force. The magnetic force of Earth makes the compass needle point north.

The compass needle spins on a thin post. Compasses have markings. They are N (north), S (south), E (east), and W (west).

The files of the United States patent office are filled with descriptions of goofy inventions. File #560,351 is for a "Device for Producing Dimples" on the face. It is made of a brace worn over the head. Attached to the brace is a "compass-directed" mechanical arm which "presses on the face in the desired spot to form a dimple."